I AM NEW ORLEANS

I Am New Orleans:
36 Poets Revisit Marcus Christian's Definitive Poem

Manufactured in the United States of America
ISBN: 978-1-60801-190-2

Cover photograph courtesy of Earl K. Long Library's
Marcus Christian Collection

Book and cover design: Alex Dimeff

Printed on acid-free paper
First edition

RUNAGATE PRESS

UNIVERSITY OF NEW ORLEANS PRESS
2000 Lakeshore Drive
Earl K. Long Library, Room 221
New Orleans, Louisiana 70148
United States
504-280-7457
unopress.org

I AM NEW ORLEANS

36 poets revisit Marcus Christian's definitive poem

edited by Kalamu ya Salaam

RUNAGATE PRESS

UNIVERSITY OF NEW ORLEANS PRESS

Contents

Foreword
Kalamu ya Salaam

This collection is a gathering of the saints. Contemporary writers with an ear to the ground, digging on the sense and sound of what all is going down. Plus, a couple of ancestor scribes, whose amazing words and clear-eyed visions remain both accurate and relevant long, long after their physical demise. Hence, here is a compendium of views and visions that collectively maps the outlines of what it means both to be and to miss New Orleans.

I woke up one morning; this project was pounding in my cranium. All I could do was respond: I hear you knocking. So, I rounded up a passel of poets, at least a few dozen or so of the ones I could easily find. Cried out, "Saddle up and let's ride!" And respond they did. Here we go. Thirty-some voices flying their identity flags high. Spy boys and gals for our dearly beloved city.

The instructions were: Say something about our town. Serious or silly. Long as a full-length seafood po-boy on lightly toasted French, garnished with tomato, lettuce, pickles, and hot sauce. Or short as a triangle-cut tuna-salad finger sandwich (with the crust sliced off the edges). Are you down for an entree of three or four soft-shell crabs with a generous portion of raisin&pineapple-laced bread pudding for dessert? After all, this is New O., where anything goes, even alligator on a stick.

Tony Jackson initiated the piano professor tradition, while Buddy Bolden was cornet-blowing the bad air out the window. A sit-down band would make a Sunday lunch complete, whilst a raucous brass band was carrying 'em away in the street. We may be internationally celebrated for jazz. Howsoever, our unique American city is not only a smorgasbord of earthly, aural, and culinary delights. We are also a multiethnic collection built on a majority base of African-heritage laborers, artisans, and intellectuals mixed with European, Latin American, and Asian elements. This collection carries on in the tradition of being a spectrum of attitudes and outlooks on the black-, brown-, and beige-hand side.

Every reality contains both positives and negatives. We celebrate the positives and work to transform the negatives. While we exclaim what we love, we do not deny that there are wrongs that seem to always remain to be righted. There is, and will always be, work to do—challenges to be faced, inequalities to be leveled, and, yes, weaknesses to be strengthened, including our own—as well as failures and limitations that we both acknowledge and fervently struggle to reverse. But, ah yes, that is the reality of all life: every day and every night has its internal and external contradictions. Within our individual selves, as well as within our society at large, there are also elements that the religious among us call "evil." But, you know, that's the way of the world (and has always been).

There are choking plants and pests in every garden. Every day we must uproot the weeds and work to eliminate the insects while we tend to the food and flowers. The ultimate reality of daily life is a roller coaster of ups and downs. Whether or not we acknowledge what's not good about New Orleans, we will always celebrate our beauty and our vitality. Yes, even in death we will dance; we will be beautiful even on our way out of life.

At the turn of this new millennium, this twenty-first century, the deepest divide all of us had to somehow navigate across was the down-pressing tumult of Katrina in late August of 2005. The resultant and long-lasting physical scars were easily perceived via the electronic media that was broadcast worldwide, displaying the overwhelming, atmospheric calamity that besotted our city. Physical markings were left behind on the wooden, stucco, brick, cement block, and glass-and-steel buildings.

Most structures still standing in the affected areas were visible cankers blotting our metropolitan landscape. However, far beyond the semi-indelible physical notations were the psychic debilitations. Although generally unseen from the outside, there was a permanent psychological patina that watermarked the emotional lives of New Orleans residents. Nevertheless, we survived the storm's emotional slaughter by obstinately vowing to keep on keeping on regardless of the crippling circumstances that time and whatever gods there be had conspired to inflict upon us.

You've heard the phrase "saints and sinners"? Well, we be both. We dance down wild streets decked out in white Communion Sunday clothes or saunter, leaning stylishly on a mahogany walking cane while sporting sky-pieces, tignons, turbans, and assorted other head gear. Greet our friends with a mutual kiss on both cheeks, cher, and cool ourselves waving hand fans with King's picture printed on them. Whether a high school marching band or some trumpet-led brass band, our pulsing music pushes us prancing and dancing on. That's the way we roll—much of our art, a public aesthetic presented to our people profiling in our streets, especially Mardi Gras Indian-feathered chanting and proud stepping or could even be hearse-encased strolling on our last go-round, heading to the great beyond.

Describe our dizzy denizens and the way that we do our do, I challenged my fellow secretaries of the spirit. No restriction on genre or form. Brief haiku or full-throated five-page rant. No matter. Pious paeans or potty-mouth screams. Just identify us for who we be. Who's the prettiest? We is!

Tell the truth, and every little thing will be alright.

Write on. Read on.

—Kalamu ya Salaam

October 2019

Marcus Christian

I Am New Orleans

I am New Orleans—
Queen City of the South;
As fabulous—as fantastic and unreal as the cities of the
Arabian Nights.

I am America epitomized:
A blending of everything—
Latin, Nordic, and Negro,
Indian, European, and American.

I inflamed the mind of John Law
And aroused his ambition and cupidity;
His partners were Avarice and Crime and Lust:
I knew Envy and Hatred, Shame and Despair.
Yet, I made them picture me then as I am now—A Dream
City—then nestling in the lap of wildernesses.

I brought souls reeling
Out of the jails and assignation houses of France,
Out of Parisian cabarets and the sleepy bourgs of far
provinces,
I herded them together upon huge ships,
Bound for the New Eldorado . . . .
Lofty ships bearing the names of great Frenchmen,
Such as *le Grand Duc du Maine*, *le Comte de Toulouse*, *le
Maréchal de Villars*, *le Dauphiné*, *le Prince de Conti*,
and *le Duc de Noailles*.

When fame outstripped the ambling winds of truth,
I stretched forth strong hands
And plucked men out of the green fields of Alsace,
Out of German beer-gardens—
Out of Mainz and Bremen, Baden and Wurttemberg;
Out of Switzerland and Spain, Ireland and England,
I brought them to my New Land of Promise.
And when the cry went forth for men—more men—to
    till my bounteous valley,
I took my vessels with resounding names
And set their sails for the Dark Continent. . . .
Murderers, salt smugglers, thieves, counterfeiters, tobacco
    smugglers, and *forçats*;
Femmes de force, *filles de joie*, and *filles à la cassette*;
German and Irish Redemptioners sold for their passage
    over and whipped like black slaves—
Black slaves sold like cattle and labeled, *pièce d'Inde:*
Such was my beginning.

Huguenots fleeing Catholics and Catholics fleeing
    Protestants;
Red Republicans fleeing Monarchists—
Proud Monarchists shunning the ominous shadow of the
    head-hungry guillotine;
Indians fleeing the stake, only to be bound as slaves;
Blacks hiding from slavery and the white world's "Thou
    Shalt Not!"
And whites in frenzied, terror-stricken flight before the
    wind-whipped fires of black rebellion.
Throughout those cruel years of hounds and hares,

My soil became a refuge for the hunted:
This was my destiny.

I saw the Ursuline Sisters with their heavy Rosaries,
Their Catechisms, and their black slaves;
I welcomed the Jesuits and the Capuchins,
Dressed in their brown-black cassocks,
And the sandalled feet of *Père* Dagobert and *Père* Antonio
    de Sedella fell softly upon me.

I am New Orleans.
Over my cobblestones and muddy byways
Have passed the *coureurs de bois*, the pioneer, the aristocrat,
    the slave, the soldier, the pirate, and the gentleman-farmer,
And they within whose veins the blood of many races mingled.

Out of the swamps of Louisiana,
Out of the blue mud and sand of the Delta,
Out of hurricanes, storms, and crevasses,
Out of Indian massacres and slave insurrections,
Phoenix-like have I risen;
Out of French, Spanish, and American dominations,
I have preserved my soul.

I have seen so many flags go up above my soil—
I have changed hands so often—
Until I have grown wise—as a woman grows wise who has
    known many lovers.

I broke the might of English sails that came
Up over the rim of the sea—

White gulls skimming before the red winds of war
But I am New Orleans;
I was not afraid . . .
I took my unwieldy elements—
Of Creoles, Americans, Frenchmen, Spaniards, Jews,
    Africans, mixed-bloods, Germans, Irishmen, and
    Indians,
And welded them into one common bond of defense
That drove the invaders back into the sea.

I have known many people—
Many voices—
Many languages.
I have heard the soft cries of the African,
Jargoning in European tongue:
"Belle desfigues!"
"Bon petit calas! Tout chauds, chere, tout chauds!"
"Pralines—pistaches! Pralines—pacanes!"
"Ah got duh nice yahlah bananas, lady!"
"Bla-a-a-a-ack ber-r-r-r-r-e-e-e-e-z!"
"Peenotsa! Peenotsa! Cuma gitta fromee!"

"Ah wanna qua'tee red beans,
  Ena qua'tee rice,
  Ena piece uh salt meat—
  Tuh makkit tas'e nice:
  En hurry up, Mr. Groceryman,
  En put dat lan-yap in mah han'!"

"Papa Bonnibee, beat dem hot licks out!—
  Ah sed, Poppa Stoppa, let dat jazz cum out!

En efyuh donh *feel* it,
'Tain't no use tellin' yuh
Jess what it's all about!
Now, gimmie sum High C's on dat horn 'n' let dem
    Saints go marching in!" . . .
"'Way Down Yonder In New Orleans."
"Take it away, Mister Charlie!"

I am New Orleans
Where plump little brown girls
With heavy-laden grocery pushcarts
Follow their double-jointed daddies around,
Good-naturedly heckling them through acres of super-
    mart goodies.
"Donh fergit now, Daddy, Mammah say tuh gittah ham-
    bone tuh put endy beans!"
"Baby, Ole Daddy ainh gonh nevah fergit nut'n lak *dat!*"
"Ahm gonh gittah hambone dat's gonh make dem stink!"
"Gonh makdy beans stink, hunh, Daddy?—Daddy sayee
    gonh makdy beans *stink!*"
"Yeah, Baby, Ole Daddy gonh gittah hambone dat'll
    make dem beans stink jess lackah ole-fashion' coun-
    try privy!"
"Un-n-n-n-h, Daddy! donh bleev Ah wanenny efdy gonh
    stink *dat* much!"

Many voices—Many languages.
I have been alternately cursed and praised in the hoarse
    gutturals of the African and the German;
I have been condemned and cajoled in the machine gun
    polysyllables of the Italian;

I have been damned and glorified
In the French of the Sorbonne, of Paris, and of the
    Communes.
I have been alternately execrated and blessed by the
    Indian, the Spaniard, and the Irishman;
Proud mulatto Creoles have cursed and excoriated me
In French and Spanish that shamed their betters—
Then wiped my dust from their disdainful feet
For star-cross'd destinies in foreign lands,
But they returned to grovel in my dust and weep;
Exiles no more, but lovers.
I have known epidemics, vicissitudes, and calamities:
    —Tar-barrels flaming at street-corners, and big guns
    barking defiance to plague-stricken air, yet Asiatic
    cholera scourged me hard in drunken, berserk fury;
    they who danced the night before died in the hush
    of dawn.
But when the cry raced forward: *"El Vomito!" "El Vomito!"*
Brave men lost courage—quitted loved ones—*fled!*

Yellow fever epidemics have left me shrivelled and shrunken;
Fires have swept through and gutted me;
Human passions have done likewise;
But after all is done,
I arise from the still warm ashes
More beautiful than ever.
Wars have played upon my heart-strings
Their symphonies of human emotions
Of love. envy, anger, malice, hatred, and greed.
Iberville, Bienville, Perrier, De Vaudreuil, Galvez, Andy
    Jackson, and Ben Butler.

Samba, the revolutionary Bambara king;
Bras Coupé, the one-armed black brigand
With a price upon his head;
The do-or-die stand of the Savarys at the Battle of New
    Orleans;
Marie Laveau, the simple-minded holy woman,
Maligned and lied upon by every passing scribbler:
Mother Catherine, whose faithful flock still awaits her
    resurrection;
And Brother Isiah, who looked like Christ and healed
    the sick and afflicted:
All these have I known.
Revolutionary hands have been lifted for and against me;
Men like Bloody O'Reilly have left their trails of human blood,
But I, in turn,
Absorbed the blood of despot and despised
And each, in turn, became a part of me.
Red hell has flamed upon my very streets
As men fought bloody duels to the death—
Where later children sang their songs at play.

* * * * *

"Green grass-tuh, green grass-tuh—how green duh grass grow!
All over, all over, it seems to be so!
Miss Walker, Miss Walker, your true love is dead;
He sent you a letter to turn back your head."

* * * * *

"Here are two gentlemen just from Spain,
 Who came to court your daughter Jane;
 Your daughter Jane she is too young
 To be control-led by anyone:
 Go back, go back, you sassy man,
 And choose the faires' in duh lan' . . ."
—"The faires' one that I can see—
 Is . . . Come, Loretta and go wid me . . ."
"Loretta is gone, Loretta is gone, widda Guinea-gold ring on
        her finger;
 Good-bye, Loretta! Good-bye, Loretta!
 We'll never see you no more."

* * * * *

Mary Mack,
Dressed in black,
Twenty-four buttons
Up and down her back.
She asked her ma
For fifteen cents
To see the elephant
Jump the fence.
He jumped so high
To the sky;
Never come back
Till next July.

* * * * *

"Swallahs, swallahs fly
Around duh yahlah house
En all duh girls on Kuh-nell Street
Is dead-'n'-gone in love
Exceptin' Miss Louisa—
And who she really loves?—
She loves Albert and Albert loves her.
With bells upon her fingers,
With bells upon her toes,
With a baby in her arms
And that's the way she goes."

* * * * *

And all the girls on Canal Street are dead-and-gone in love!
Listen to them sing!
Waiting on the levee,
Waiting for the steamboat coming 'round the bend;
Waiting for the *Pargoud*—
Waiting for the *Natchez*—
Waiting for the *Robert E. Lee*—

"Ah gotta man on duh *Pargo'*;
Ah gotta man on duh *Lee*;
Ah gotta man on duh *Natchez*;
En he's comin' wid money fuh me—
En he's comin' wid money fuh me."

Sing, O, my children, sing!
Sing of a day that long was,
And fondly remembered, still is,

But can never come back again!
Let one long keening ride the wayward winds and spend
    itself on yonder hills and valleys.

So come now, little childun,
Cuz you done had yo' day:
Come, set down heah wid Grandpa,
Hit's nigh tuh close o' day.
Compair Lapin, Compair Bouki,
Wonh be wid us tunight,
Cuz we's tiahed o' ole Brer Rabbit—
Now tell me, aint dat right?

Done tole yall all dem bedtime tales,
So, on dis night A'n means
Tuh sing tuh yall uh nice li'l song
'Bout good ole New Awleans.

"In sebenteen-eighteen it wuz foun'
W'en Ben Ville sailed in safe en soun'
Wid fifty mens tuh clear duh groun'
E-eye-e-eye-O! (String it out with a long gravy.)
E-eye-e-eye-O!" (Now a lightning-fast yodel.)

"He kumd bout thuh middle o' Febuwary,
Jess fo' duh rivah cud git cuntrary
En flood duh lan' en duh tremblin' prairie."

"Now, duh rich mens' wives wuz proud en col'
En dey dress'd in satin, silk, en gol'
But duh maidens fair wuz brash en bol'."

"Sum wuz skinny en sum wuz fat.
 En dey walked lak dis en dey walked lak dat;
 But dey'd all kiss uh man at duh drappin' o' uh hat;"

"'Twas back in 1781
 W'en Galvez kumd wid his big gun,
 En capchud ev'y Englishman.
 Agin dey tried tuh tek duh town!
 But Andy Jackson he kumd down
 En rund 'em en duh rivah en made 'em drown!"

"So, lock up duh cabin—th'ow out duh greens—
 Put on duh calico en yahlah jeans,
 En let's go down tuh New Awleens . . . ."

I am New Orleans—
A perpetual Mardi Gras
of wild Indians, clowns, lords and ladies,
Bourbon Street Jezebels, Baby Dolls, and Fat Cats;
Peanut-vendors, flower-sellers, organ-grinders, chimney-
     sweepers, and fortune-tellers,
And then, at the end, bone-rattling skeletons and flying ghosts.

I am New Orleans—
A city that is a part of, and yet apart from all America;
A collection of contradictory environments;
A conglomeration of bloods and races and classes and colors;
Side-by-side, the New tickling the ribs of the Old;
Cheek-by-jowl, the Ludicrous making faces at the Sublime.

Here, in the graceful curve of Ole Man Mississippi,
Where the lazy old Father of the Waters
Meanders down to the gulf,
I sing my song:
I sing the song of the Siren, the Voluptuary, the Sybarite;
Here, within this ever-green valley and under warm tropical
    skies,
Where guitars tinkle softly deep in a moonlit night
And softer voices whisper of my beauty,
I sing of the newest phases of my greatness;
Reveling in the quickening of Progress within and around me,
    I sing of the bewildering expanses
of far-reaching bridges and overpasses;
I sing of glittering cities of the sky thrusting themselves
    up from the Delta mud,
Brushing the clouds of heaven
With dreams of Recilian beauty and grace;
I sing of far vistas of asphalt streets and highways
Beckoning us on to fantastic future years;
I sing of the Past, the Present, and the boundless Future;
I sing of Love, Adventure, and Enchantment.

Sing, O, my children, sing!
Sing of a day that long was,
And fondly remembered, still is,
But can never come back again!

Nia Gates, *written at age thirteen*

My Neighborhood Is Changing

my neighborhood is changing
everything rearranging
i write it down
every word and every sound

to remember how it was
and what it will be
one day my neighborhood
won't be mine
because in time
new people will come and go
and my neighborhood will change slow
i will have to leave
because it won't be mine anymore

i take pictures of my neighborhood now
so in the future i will remember
what it was
and i can see what it is

i write and capture to remember
so the new people can see
what it used to be
my neighborhood will change
and rearrange
some see the best
others are blind like the rest

they can't tell
even if you ring a bell
they can't see
that it's about to flee
that the lower nine
won't be mine
because a new will come
i don't know where from
but nothing will be the same
except for the frame

but the picture a new
a different crew
my neighborhood is soon to be gone
life will move on
home is where the heart is they say
well my heart will rot and decay
because the lower nine won't be the same
what a shame
so many lives have been built here
and in the end, get torn down
home becoming a green space
such a disgrace
how can they make grounds to play
if the people don't have a place to stay
the man with the money
always actin' funny
they say it's for our health
but they are doing it for their wealth
money comes out of our pockets
while his wealth rockets

they want new parks
where dogs can bark
but the lower nine is changing
and rearranging
i can't tell is it better or worse
the people can't even buy their own hearse
i am trying to say
are we getting played
in this game
they want the money and the fame
they are the piece
we are the board
getting stepped on lives crushed
and dreams flushed
is that it
does this piece fit

in the modern age
and this is just a stage
because more changes will come
and the beat of another drum
look around
no words or sounds
nothing can replace the lower nine
because it's a unique design
but they're making a new blue print
which will leave a dent
in what New Orleans is
and forever will be
but now you can see
it isn't just me

we are all one family
the lower nine
is a place that can't be replaced
people will come and go
and the buildings will fall
but in my heart
and everyone who was here from the start
the real lower nine shall stay
and we will pray
that one day
it will come back
the lower nine is a glass of fine wine
something you don't want to waste
after the first taste

Karen Celestan

Blood Nativity

I.

Always felt the river
lapping whispers of my elders' tears
in every wave that slapped the rocks.
The breeze calls from sugar cane fields up 90
where grandmother entered life, losing her mother
as she shook off the placenta.
The rhythmic speech that sang with cadences
of West Africa, drum beats of love, innate will,
            everlasting power of Ibo tribes.

II.

Walking to the Algiers ferry
calmed me, linking heart to sweaty blues.
Saying 'hey, now' to Frogman,
his recognition smile—'you a Victor, right?'—
boggy voice asking about Tootsie, my mama and 'nem.

III.

Hopping off the Claiborne bus, clutching a thin-paper NOPSI transfer
to get a po-boy at Levata's after class,
fresh-peeled shrimp hot out the grease from cast iron of the ages.
Old creole man peering over black-rimmed, thick glasses
to talk about everythang and nuttin'
savoring every bite of the crisp, buttered loaf
bathed in ketchup and 'that hot stuff.'

IV.

Sitting shaded under those solid oaks on Gentilly Boulevard
          content
with two other Karens, Dana, Carol and Lauren
as Michael O. Williams seduced us with guitar riffs,
his gleaming, uniform teeth alighting his glabrous umber skin
          all 18, with life's maybes racing through our heads.

V.

Strong uncle hugs, everything from four aunties' stoves,
    Mother's pancakes.
A family multitude, breeding strength and security through
    elders' fears.
Neighborhood folks speaking and door-poppin'. Crawfish and
    beer. Dances at the ILA.
Ancestors touching my face through searing sunlight,
Holding this young spirit aloft in preparation and solicitation
        to battle
every strata of plantation mentality.

Jerry W. Ward, Jr.

Genders & Genres
(law's labor loses love)

Middle passages
of hurricanes—
death borne by birth
in a poem
elusive
inconclusive—
enigma eternal.
Retell, retail
a lie
into reliability.
Muddle passages
of hurricanes—
birth borne by death
in a romance
complicates
duplicates—
enslavements internal.
Fornicate a fib
into a fable.
"The theory of America
let freedom prove
no man's inalienable
right! Every one
who can tyrannize,
let her tyrannize
to his satisfaction!"
Distract distraction

into

denial.

Muddle middle passages

of hurricanes—

future drama of ancient rain

trauma

incarcerate

a lie

in perfect deniability.

"The theory of America—

hurricanes let nothing remain upon the earth except the ashes."

Fires have swept through and gutted me;

Human passions have done likewise...

JB Borders

We

We the half-made denizens of this not-so-ancient port
We the stranded
The intoxicated
The inebriated
Satiated
Subordinated
Giddy and ungainly
Ungainful even to ourselves
Our own swellness

Deployed in this realm of decrepitude
For mute and ever mournful toil
Toting, hoeing, sewing, stewing, brewing, blowing, mopping,
    chopping, painting,
feinting, digging, jigging, grinning and grinning some more

Let swill, tabac, musique and grub drain away
The resentment
The merely quenchable inclination to revolt and rule

Let swamps be cleared for the expansion of commerce
For Lebensraum
Beside the Mesachabe
In the armpit of Dixie
A nigger yard or two
Tucked neatly in the wholes of some consumptive scheme/
    dream to transcend
zoomanity

The recurring urge to corner, kill, cook
To domesticate and routinize

Giddy and ungainly
Ungainful even to ourselves
Our own swellness
Subordinated
Satiated
In this not-so-ancient port
Oui
Wee
We
All the way home

Kelly Harris-DeBerry

Post-Katrina Blues

ribbon cuttings
can almost make you
forget

black bodies shot on
danziger bridge

henry glover
burned

skull still missing

a new city
a new year

makes neighborhoods look
rebuilt

zoom in closer

lift the headlines
rent rose higher

than the waterlines

still coughing
from chinese dry wall

and FEMA trailers

housing and home
ain't the same thing

it ain't easy no more
it millennials

walking their dogs
in their purses

transplants complaining
about loud jazz

and correcting southern
pronunciations

Super Bowls
can make you forget

donations spent
to attract people far far away

wanting your smile
for their pictures

they selfie you without permission
and want to pet your hair

order you like a cold drink
and ask you to twerk

for their research
all this new can make you forget

how talk like that dat
and dem and all the peoples

we be before it was New
better for whom?

families can't afford to stay
in their new

old neighborhoods
where they've always been

this new can make you forget

the smell of sitting water
and feces and the dead

that never saw the new coming
a black president can make you forget

Bush and trick eyes
into believing we are post-racial

milestones can be mind games
old ways still the same

pre-K to post-K
plantation education

left every child under
blankets of greed

tucked them into poison
homeless beg and shake

a saints cup and yells
we won

who screams for the hungry

and the bellhop
serving a silver smile

on a tarnished platter
who eats and whose hands rot

the land. Where's the X
on the front pages

where politicians kiss babies
and smear lies on their cheeks

how many left?
how many po-boys

can make you forget da poor
and who makes the bread

who slices us a piece of
ourselves and hires

our genius at minimum wage
gotta dance to keep from crying

can't see my face in the new

shiny buildings can make you forget
slow love and porch talks

and sweet tea and borrowed sugar
and families who knew your

grandma and 'nem
Katrina anniversaries

can make you leave
New Orleans
for Detroit

or the next New
maybe I'm new too

got to remember how
to rescue myself

cause all this new
still leaves me waiting

in a long line for help

Marian Moore

Martha

$10 REWARD,
Will be paid to any person who will bring to No. 27 Tchoupitoulas st., a Negro Girl, about 13 years of age—very dark, ruff skin, quite sprightly, and wears a blue cottonade dress; she is of rather short stature; her name is *Martha*, and she absented herself on the 24th of November.   nov 29 31

I shucked that dress
Found two ears of corn
clinging to a gunnysack on the docks
Enough to stop my gullet's teeth
from chewing through my rough skin
The bag an easy fit.
Last night rolled myself in dog shit.
Enough to make the pretty noses
and the sharp eyes
above them
turn away
from my burlap slip
Replaced cottonade—
that weft of Louisiana cotton with
a warp of Tennessee jute printed
in indigo
The color
staining my thin thighs
purple
with the blood of my kin
red
embracing the work of their hands
blue.

Nadir Lasana Bomani

The Last Days
(My Uncle Michael Remembers)

Didn't know water could rise that fast
Didn't know I could scale a 2-story house either
Helicopter got me off the roof
Like taxis, boats weren't coming in our part of Uptown
Man asked me to hold on tight
Tell ya the truth nephew, I still haven't let go

It was the BOOM that brought some of us out of the house
We kicked on neighbor's doors like bored little boys
One Brother asked me: "Why are you yelling FIRE,
When there's so much water coming out the street?!"
My Grandma Ruth used to say,
"If you want folks to come out their house, yell FIRE
Cuz nobody coming on their porch for no HELP!"

The I-10 wasn't built for this
I've seen everything from this bridge
Except a cloud
We wait for buses to take us somewhere
American
Where folk don't season their beans

Who will second line for New Orleans once the people are gone?

I stare at the still waters below
Thinking of all the good music I lost down there
That double album Stevie won a Grammy for
Was the first time I saw a blind man cry

That's when I broke down.

Mwende "FreeQuency" Katwiwa

Ode to ~~New Orleans~~Home

"home is not where you are born;
home is where all your attempts
to escape cease"
——Naguib Mahfouz

I.
and when I came to you
mid escape
suitcases unclasped
baggage spilling out of every seam

i was 18 years searching
18 years not finding or being found
18 years of doubt and displacement
of being taken from and to
my next home
and my next home
and my next home
and my next home
and my next home
till I forgot that home
had meaning beyond movement
beyond the in between
beyond grasping for memories
too shallow to settle into facts of the past

you were the first place that (I) felt familiar in the foreign

the first place that asked me to let go
you told me the river could handle my load
and only in the release did I realize
how much hurt i'd held through the hollowing

II.
when I was a teenager,
my mother said,
"new orleans reminds me of home"

for years
she echoed in my ears
and searching heart
until I stepped foot in this village
and saw chickens directing traffic
like arrogant, well dressed crossing guards

until I tried to refuse a meal
only for the plate to be piled higher
with the same expectation
it would come back clean

until I walked out of a house
timid and tentative
to find myself swirled
in the chaos of joy
that is a Sunday street
in New Orleans

III.
but it wasn't just the second lines
it was the second chance
at home
the first chance   .
to choose it

i didn't know
what I was walking into
but for the first time
in a long time
i decided i wanted
to keep walking
forward and toward
like I had just realized that
life was a gathering of the living
and my invitation had been waiting for me
right here all along

Proud mulatto Creoles have cursed and excoriated me

In French and Spanish that shamed their betters—

Then wiped my dust from their disdainful feet

For star-cross'd destinies in foreign lands,

But they returned to grovel in my dust and weep...

Mawiyah Kai EL-Jamah Bomani

color

we had all kinds of names for them black black black chillun
what use to try and entertain us 7th ward creole chillun
you know anybody was too black to be cute
was curious bout life
  on the other side of the fence
  it's true
if they denying it
then they talking horse shit
  and you betta get out the way
  fore some land in your eyes
we use to be harder on them darkies worse than them white folks
cause we had the privilege of knowing everything bout their kin
most times they had a mama or aunty or nanny
that worked under one of our relatives
doing some days work while our relatives tended to the white folks
    chillun
it wasn't like back in slavery times what with all that forced
    breastfeeding
by pickaninny house servants
no wasn't that at all
see slavery had long since been abolished
so us creoles were looked upon as special exotic
everyone had to manifest just one cause we didn't throw the decorum
    off tilt
being in the presence of one of us who had the fortune of passing
was extremely special
the cream of the crop kinda special
special cause we could get close to white folk's chillun

special cause you know white folks don't just entrust the care
and maintenance of their offspring to anybody
I mean we'd carry them chillun to the market
and walk them round the neighborhood
when they was colicky and restless
nobody would second guess
that the child wasn't with its rightful owner or related kin
that's exactly why we had to run them darkies
whenever they tried to come round to play
so happens that was always
after the baptist church let out on sunday
our secrets had to remain hushed
we was catholic simply cause
my grandmamma said
the surest way to tell your true color
is to go serving at that baptist church round the way
with all them midnight colored folk
clowning like a jungle worth of baboons for the lawd
making him tone deaf when it comes to orderly worship like ours
white folks catch you creeping out them nigger baptist churches and it
wouldn't take long fore you branded a pasty nigger
on account of your niggerish actions on account of the company
        you keep
anyhow time church was out some of them jiggaboos, tar babies,
        soot bellies, burnt biscuits,
midnights, ink spots, blue blacks, sambos would enter our neck of
        the woods we'd unleash all them names along with rocks trying
        to split their heads
just to see if the black had infiltrated their blood
my cousin Joe said that one drop of an ink spot's blood
would turn you black in a manner of seconds

and from then on your chillun would be born
looking like they belonged on planet of the apes
I asked my grandpapa and he swore Joe was as right as the sky is blue
so when you aiming aim right at their skull
try to almost kill 'em teach 'em Judith
we's pure and they kind and our kind got nothing in common
this color this creole hue
gal has erased what use to be intertwined history
our creole history begins at this moment
look at these wars
like battles for independence
by any means necessary Judith
we aiming for split justice

Niyi Osundare

New Orleans Is People

New Orleans is
Humanity, Music, and Desire

New Orleans is
Agriculture, Piety, and Abundance

New Orleans is
Art, Felicity, and Fidelity

New Orleans is
Treme, Bourbon, and Congo Square

New Orleans is
Wildair, Warrington, and Wickfield

New Orleans is
Pelican, Heron, and Flamingo

New Orleans is
Charity, Gentilly, and Saratoga

New Orleans is
Black Street, White Street, and Gray Boulevard

New Orleans is
Gumbo, Jambalaya, and Red Beans 'n Rice

New Orleans is
Juice, jive, and jolly jazz

New Orleans is
River, Lake, and Gulf

New Orleans is
Sounds, Saints, and Sinners

New Orleans is
Love, tears, and laughter

New Orleans is
People

Christine "Cfreedom" Brown

When You Think of New Orleans:
(Who, What, When, Where, Why, & How)

Who do you think of when you think of New Orleans?

The culture bearers or the gentrifiers

The natives or the colum-busters

The Who Dat Nation or the Saints

The pre-Katrina teachers or post-Katrina TFAers

The scholars or the dollars

Who do you think of?

It better be   the Indians and the secondliners.

It better be   the writers, storytellers, singers, rappers, musicians, and dancers.

It better be

My mama nem and yo mama nem

It better be People like Carol Bebelle and Mama Jen

Tank and the Bangas and Dee-1

Sunni Patterson and Nana Anoa

People like   Louis Armstrong, Mahalia Jackson,

Trombone Shorty, and Germaine Bazzle

Marie Laveau and Tootie Montana

It better be   the artists, healers, doulas, conjurers, organizers,
      and freedom
fighters.

It better be   the cooks and bartenders with them rouxs and
      brews; they be
some of the best chemists in this nation.

It better be   the elders and the youth from generations and
      generations;
before and after.

Time after time.   You better be thinkin' bout me and mines.

What do you think of when you think of New Orleans?

The breaching of the levees or Hurricane Katrina public
      education or
charter school systems

Gumbo or Po-boys Bounce, Poetry, or Jazz

Sweating to dat beat or sweating to dat heat What do you think of?

It better be   the removal of them statues; 133 years of evil
    worshipping
seized.

It better be   years of intergenerational organizing in these
    streets.

It better be   spiritual works and carrying on traditions and
    freedom
missions.

It better be   homeschools and new minds being cultivated and
nurtured   and lit torches being passed down from elders to
    the youth.

It better be mothers and fathers and communities uniting

And teaching the children the truth.

It better be   Misbelief Trees and seed-planting for the future to
    bear the fruit.

Time after time   You better be thinkin' bout Me and mine.

When do you think of New Orleans, when you think of New
Orleans?

Before or After the Hurricane

Hurricane, Festival, or Crawfish Season

Red Beans Mondays or Mardi Gras Fat Tuesdays

Jazz Market Wednesdays or Blue Nile Thursdays

Tipping Point or True Brew Fridays

Club Caribbean or Maafa Saturdays

Ebony Square, Congo Square, Superdome, or Secondline Sundays?

It better be   when you're spending your money to support the arts, black
businesses, community spaces, and entrepreneurs.

It better be   when you're being a positive role model to the youth in our
community, speaking and teaching at schools.

It better be   when you're raising your children and others and investing in
their future.

It better be   when you're keeping your family house in the family instead of
selling out to gentrification.

It better be   when you're buying the block and not selling rocks.

It better be   when you hit them election polls and vote

And make more opportunities for success in our community
    than to sell
dope.

It better be   when you're volunteering and donating to
    organizations in our
neighborhood.   It better be all the time!

Time after time

You better be thinkin' bout

Me and Mine.

Where do you think of when you think of New Orleans?

Below sea level or the bottom of the map

The Dirty South or Gulf of Mexico

Lake Pontchartrain or the Mississippi River

Cross the Canal or On the Bayou

City Park or Audubon

Congo Square or Jackson

The East, Bywater, or Marigny

Upper or Lower 9

Uptown, Downtown, or Backatown

Old Algiers, Across the River

Central City, Mid City, or Gentilly

Canal Street or Bourbon

Circle Food Store and Armstrong Park

Oretha Castle Haley and Martin Luther King Jr. Blvd; two ancestors
intersecting never went so hard

Where do you think of?

It better be   in the heart and soul of this nation

It better be   in Africa and in the Caribbean

It better be   Angola prison where they incarcerate the most
      people in the
world

It better be   in the spirit of our Ancestors

Those that came before us and continue to live through us and our
harvests and our seeds

Time after time   You better be thinkin' bout Me and Mine.

Why do you think of New Orleans, when you think of New Orleans?

Is it because of the Saints Or Drive Thru Daiquiris

Is it because of twerking and dropping it like it's hot

Is it because of Cash Money and No Limit Lil Wayne or Master P

Is it because of parades, partying and bullshitting any given
    day of the
week

Festivals and concerts all year round

Or is it because it is sacred grounds?

Is it because of tourism

And Southern Hospitality

Good Food and 24/7

Liquor   Historic buildings and antiques

Abandoned homes and building and lands

Cheap cost of living and investing for you but high priced for
    me and my
family

Gentrification, the modern day segregation

Minimum wage and poverty, the modern day slavery

Is it because of capitalism

The prison capital of the world

And failing school systems

Being the same business

Same architects, engineers, CEOs, wardens, and principals

Is it because it was the principle slave port of this country

And if you black in America then you most likely have
ancestral roots here

Or if you white in America then you might have some
misdirected fear

Why do you think of New Orleans?

Because of Dooky Chase and Willie Mae's

Because of the Angola Three and the Black Panther Party

Because of the Mother-in-Law Lounge and Secondline Sundays

Because of Jazz Funerals and Ancestor Trees

Because Mardi Gras Indians and soul food cooking

Because of Treme, the oldest black neighborhood in the country

Because of Treme, Community Book, and Ashé Cultural Arts
    Center

Because ain't no other place like New Orleans in this country.

Closest places like it, you gotta travel across seas.

Places like Cuba, Haiti, Jamaica, St. Lucia, and many African
    countries

Because it's a combination of several cultures with Spanish and
    French
influences

But African blood and roots

Because it's in your DNA and your ancestors keep calling you.

The real question is HOW could you not Think of New Orleans?

Time after time   You can't help but think 'bout

Me and mine.

Asali Ecclesiastes

1201 Ursulines

a lavender and grey shotgun,
trimmed and eight-foot fenced
in sherwin williams' caribbean blue
resides at the corner
of ursulines and st. claude;
inside is high and wide
when stepping thru the threshold
there is a lull between realities
as you are shelled
of your outside self;
whoever you have to be
in the streets to survive
stays on the porch
where a sun-bleached red chair sits,
a place of rest for personas;
the rest of you enters
into a space of unfolding
where beauty is pursued forcefully and gloom is not withstood
for it is overstood, mood is matter;
its crafters were careful to fashion
doorways tall enough to welcome giant spirits
its dwellers were devoted to
keeping them there
for beside sidewalks crammed
with banana trees
honeysuckle and sunflowers,
fig trees, lime trees,
mint, gardenia, and night-blooming jasmine bushes,
run streets lush with blood——guts and tyranny

the city signs say tremé
but the "banquet" defies,
cries LIBERTY;
children feed equally on the fruits
of "mispaleaf" and mis-belief
misery often overflowing into households
and in the flood zone
sometimes it never stops rising;
so every sunday for two seasons
the village communes
to beat it stomp it dance it jump it sing it moan it
chant it shout it drum it sousaphone trombone trumpet it
back into the ruts, furrows, and potholes
left by dragging tour busses
and racing patrol cars;
and at our address
we paint red, yellow, turquoise, and orange walls;
we hang paintings, posters, pictures of indian suits, and instruments;
we cook fried fish, jambalaya, yat-ka-mein, and cowain
we play jazz, gospel, reggae, hip-hop, and spades;
we make groceries, furniture, families, and sense;
we make music, clothes, businesses, and arguments
we make drinks, rent, festivals, and clubs;
we make jewelry, grass roots institutes, poems, and love

and regardless of who is sitting
on the sofa in the front room,
be it pusher, politician, pastor, or policeman—
or any of the good or bad people they oppress—
all can converse soul to soul;
we make friends with neighbors
we make home.

Baakir Tyehimba

A Battle for Algiers

It's a gang of guerrillas poised for expressive thoughts
In what was once the training grounds for the architects of Free Town

It's a maroon camp of black cats who vow never to bow
To none other than themselves
And then, only with love and reverence

Some of 'em said it had to be the closer parts of the caves of West Asia
No less than the land of dark faces across the waters
They calculated that it had to be Algeria

A little like Afraka. Full of Afrakans
A great small world of interdependent, interconnected families
    where Freedom and Power meet
Where we want for our families what we want for ourselves

It's some bad brothas and sistas in my comrade's house
Spooky and frightenin where these guerrilla cats get together with
    cause
They've been born to destroy what ain't
And build what is… Little Afraka

In the Westbank of the Crescent City

Out of the swamps of Louisiana,

Out of the blue mud and sand of the Delta,

Out of hurricanes, storms, and crevasses,

Out of Indian massacres and slave insurrections,

Phoenix-like have I risen...

Carol Bebelle

Letter to New Orleans

My Dear New Orleans,

All my life, you have been my touchstone, the place where I fit in and belong.

I know the cadence of your heartbeat and the rhythm of your streets,

My Dear New Orleans.

You have shown me life so sweet, it brings joy to my heart and life so hard it makes me cry.

I have learned balance and how to keep it in the New Orleans equation that offers such a wonderful blend of culture, art, lifestyle, spirit and just plain living.

These values prevail and continue to thrive, despite the drag and resistance of absent social justice, missing fairness and equal access that are so required to meet the quality-of-life promise that is yours to grab.

Dear New Orleans, you have shown the world the need to enjoy the fullest range of human experiences from birth to death.

You help populate the human landscape with notice and ritual that reminds us of the true value of living.

My Dear New Orleans, you are rising from a beat-down disaster that would have destroyed most, and are singing away your blues, dancing up a storm of revival while you take leap after leap of faith that, around a near corner, across an overpass, or up a familiar street, a new New Orleans waits for us all.

And, we are becoming stronger, wiser, better and more hopeful as we see progress marching down streets like a Sunday Secondline.

Wave after wave of folks are joining, as the rhythm passes by and the brass band's echo is calling the still-away home.

My Dear New Orleans, we are intending ourselves into a new tomorrow where everyone has a good place to live, a decent job, lifelong education and great health care that assures wellness and safety that transforms our fear into vital energy.

New Orleans, we are finding a new willingness and new ways to work outside our comfort zone, with each other, to create a new zone of wellbeing for everyone.

My Dear New Orleans, I was born here, I live my life here and this is where I will someday die. Add me to the looooong list of New Orleans believers, well-wishers and mojo makers, who are wanting, working, praying and willing you into a new era of New Orleans brilliance!

Blessings and Best Wishes
From Your Forever Daughter
Carol

Author's Commentary

This letter to New Orleans, written and read for NPR in 2009, has been recorded and made part of Ashé Cultural Arts Center's CD, *Healing Force*, produced in collaboration with local producer/writer Kalamu ya Salaam and master drummer/producer Luther Gray. It is available through a variety of digital music services.

Today, January 2018, the observations of the poem still ring true. Our accomplishments, thirteen years forward, have been driven by a passion to take advantage of the rebuilding opportunity that resulted from the 2005 flood disaster known as "Katrina." The fact that the opportunity was made possible by such dramatic human sacrifice calls us to measure progress by a different standard.

How improved are things for historical residents? How much opportunity exists for the underutilized and undeveloped talent of men and women living at or below the poverty level?

Is everyone home who wants to be? Is there a civic will rising to affect the political will toward reshaping policy and law to include everyone at the table of promise and opportunity? Does the "WE" that we claim today in our everyday speaking translate in our minds and hearts to the true diverse community/city we call New Orleans today?

Ten years later, our eyes must temper the vision of new buildings, new homes in new neighborhoods with the many new faces we see, to allow ourselves the opportunity to experience the worry and sense of missing that should force questions about those who are not present. Where did our neighbors land? How are they doing here at home, as well as in many distant places?

How could we be magnetic enough to attract so many to our crippled, devastated, down-and-out existence and not be powerful enough to be featured ourselves as part of our own recovery? The new New Orleans is still becoming, and we all must do our best to assure that it is a prophetic example of how to create a true Twenty-First Century American City.

The story of "Us" today must weave a stronger narrative of "WE." Today's New Orleans must hold a higher standard than the familiar "My Brother's Keeper." James Joseph, United States ambassador to South Africa at the birth of democracy there, reminds us that keeping our Brother or our Sister is not a relationship of equity. It does not allow for our Brother or Sister to be self-determining. It creates an uncomfortable inequity between us. It allows us to grow feelings, though often unintentional, of marginalization, indifference, and superiority.

Ambassador Joseph tells us, we want instead to be our Brother's Brother or our Sister's Sister. It is this view of each other that will allow us to weave a "WE" consciousness that dismisses the notion of a city that doesn't assure support and services for children and elders. This "WE" consciousness will recognize that the sturdiness of the economy and security for all is tied to assuring that the opportunity for livable wages, affordable housing, healthcare, and education are available for all. This "WE" consciousness will be intolerant of a criminal justice system that egregiously incarcerates young people, especially targeting those of color, depriving them of life, liberty, and the pursuit of happiness.

This new New Orleans is both aspirational and intentional in its efforts to create a city worthy of the title Model American City.

Finally, and importantly, our efforts to rebound from this disaster were made possible by the largest humanitarian response in the history of the world. This outpouring of humanity calls us to be accountable for not only recovery but renaissance as well.

We remember the lives that were lost, the sacrifices made, and the unending prayers and acts of generosity and kindness our worldwide community of neighbors made on our behalf. This must be an embedded reminder that "to those whom much is given, much is required."

My Dear New Orleans, rise and lead the way into a new era of New Orleans brilliance steeped in culture, community, commerce, civility, equity, opportunity, and joy! To do less than this is unacceptable and destines us to a future that is absent of the core ingredients necessary for a livable, viable, equitable, contemporary American City! We must be clear in our appreciation of the diverse present and future we are living. We must create a perspective, a philosophy, and a practice of being a New Orleanian that charges us with meeting this new standard of civic and social practice and lifestyle that supports a political will for equity and justice in all ways possible.

Those of us who are ready should be in stride, encouraging the reluctant ones along. Those who defiantly resist this vision for the future risk being the cause for the downfall of an American City with valuable lessons to teach to the body American.

Who do you choose to be?

Frederick "Hollywood" Delahoussaye

The Soul of NO

You are the soil where souls
find the strength to stand
your garden hardened with thoughts of magnolias and bourbon
your seeds sprouting across the globe
and even when your bowl overflowed
the gumbo wasn't too spicy to keep us from wanting more
so we feast on your false beliefs
shout up at southern skies to shower us
with voodoo and moonshine
and the strength of little boys on street corners
with Sammy Davis stems pounding pavements
while tourists find it funny
and children run after purposely un-aimed nickels
dancing down sidewalks

we love you with an ignorant curiosity
brushing your lips with only the hint of a kiss
commitment-less carnivores
whoring out your soul for doubloons, beads and kickbacks
its dreams we lack
so we drown in tears and floodwaters
swimming through deception and lies
shoulder high compromise
and bring New Orleans back commissions
but this be southern living
them closing schools and building prisons
confusion our new religion

got the billboards to prove it
lost hearts in heavy movement
but soul you are worth fighting for
so I give you my words
for you have inspired me
to aspire to be just a part of your history
your memories paved with
spirits of greatness
that even the great flood couldn't erase
I am part of you soul
left to die by those on high
for somewhere between the water-line and the color-line
lies the poverty line, so we stand in line
for shelter, safe-haven and overdue reparations
but patience wears thin when all hope is done
and I know all white boy presidents aren't crazy
but I can think of one
through politics they stay connected
the people unprotected
the wetlands still neglected
as you get dissected to the highest bidders
oh how I long to hold you soul
but arms grow weak like levees
hearts stay heavy with thoughts of tomorrow
for the city that care forgot
a governmental plot blamed on mother nature's fury
vision blurry from media blasts
of downbeat broadcasts
and a circumstance they could never understand
no name reporters becoming famous off our faults
famous off our loss

put New Orleans on a cross and crucify
they quick to catch the close-up and watch your children die

evacuee slash poet
refugee slash musician
constituent slash looter
survivor slash sinner
American citizen slash great grandson of a former slave
dancing in Congo Squares and raised graves in Treme
to African drums and brass bands
speaking in tongues with Indian chants
I'm fading from rooftops and superdomes
I'm screaming for help just craving for home
to me you are more than just a mardi gras mambo
more than blackened catfish and gumbo
you are that jazz song I heard
the night I realized music could move me
you are the muse of Cajun moons
mixed with the heat of southern humidity
you are the birthplace of civil rights
you're the reason why I write
you're the night I made all my wrongs
and the morning I tried to make them right
you're the spirit of 7th ward hard heads
buried under 17th street canals
you are the song of 100,000 strong
from uptown to the east
they're still begging to come home
so know that I won't leave you soul
I won't throw you to the wolves
and watch them tear you to pieces

I can't give you back to those who couldn't keep you
I will gather your children from across this land
for you are the soil where souls find the strength to stand
New Orleans you are not just where I live
You are who I am...

Valentine Pierce

Home

When I recall growing up in New Orleans,
I remember the foods and flavors, the fun times and funerals.
The images are vivid—bright, flickering stars.

Sunday afternoons were best, the ones when Momma had
     money
and the candy man would come. She'd buy us Crackerjacks.
Don't know the cost. What it cost didn't mean anything to me
     then.
Crackerjacks, two boxes she'd cut in half.
Don't know how she remembered
from one good Sunday to the next
who got the prize last, but she did.
Or, if the money was low, firecracker jawbreakers
that puffed out our cheeks and stung our tongues.

Saturday afternoons were good, too,
those that followed Friday nights' foot tracings
on brown paper bags
used to size eight pairs of shoes
without eight pairs of feet dragging along
'cause Momma always came back with bags of popcorn,
fresh, almost hot even, after the slow bus ride back
from Canal Street.

So were Saturday nights on a brick sidewalk, right after dusk
when street lights turned our olive-toned skin lavender

and our dark lips deep, dull purple
and we would run and play tag
with a stop sign for home base
and we'd try not to drop soft cone ice cream,
its milky white yellowed by the light.

I remember the day King was buried
how we all had to come inside and watch it on T.V.—
a long procession of people,
walking that slow way sad people walk
when their hearts are too heavy to carry.
Or was that Kennedy? No, must have been King
'cause when Kennedy died
my grandmother was watching General Hospital;
my first baby sister was only four days old.
I can't really remember because I was only four
and such things had no meaning for me then.
And when my uncle Emmanuel died:
the one who looked like wrinkled, roasted pecan shells,
the one who gave us that tiny record player
with the donut-sized records,
the one who smoked that stinky cigar.
I never understood why they kissed dead people.
Dead people can't feel, can they?

When my grandmother died
my second baby sister was only two weeks old.
Momma said it was as though she was waiting,
waiting for the baby to be born.
Momma thought she'd have trouble with my first baby sister
and my big brother, who were like grandmother's shadows,

the ones who went with her to mass every Friday evening,
who'd scream and cry every time she left the house,
but they went on like nothing had changed.

I remember one night I looked out the window
and saw my grandmother's face.
Guess I would have been scared if I had thought about it,
but I wasn't. I figured she was just keeping an eye on us.

My grandmother, she knew things nobody knew.
Like the day she asked us who put soap on her icebox.
(Sometimes I still call the refrigerator an icebox, too).
Someone had decided to use a bar of Ivory soap as a crayon
and her icebox as a chalkboard.
She said she knew who but wanted us to tell her.
I didn't know. And I didn't know how she knew.
How could anybody see white soap on a white icebox?

My grandmother could really cook.
You ever have rice pudding?
You know what *cowain* is?
Sometimes I can still taste her brown gravy and rice.
Hey, did you know parsley cures everything?
What it don't fix, some home-grown mint tea leaves will,
if you steep 'em right. My grandma knew that.
Guess that's why I'm not the sickly kind.

Rainy days were no fun with grandma—
especially with the thunder and lightning.
She would turn everything off in the house,
spread that old green and brown quilt on the floor

and make us go to sleep.
She would tell us God was mad at the world.
Me, I used to peep out our wide floor-length window
and watch the raindrops
make spinning jacks on the brick sidewalk.
My mother was the best jacks player ever!
You ever play jacks with your mom?
Mine was the champ and she taught me so well
only one child in the whole neighborhood could beat me,
and he was a boy!

Do you remember hurricane Betsy's wrath?
I don't but I remember the nightmare Betsy gave me
of dead fish and dead people floating through our house.
I do remember my mother struggling to keep her balance
in a house that rocked and shook, rocked and shook.
And I remember a man walking knee-deep in water
carrying us through a pitch black night.
I must have been asleep 'cause it still seems like a dream.
It is only through history books that I truly know Betsy's reality.

And my uncle Joe; nobody called him Joe.
Momma called him Brother.
We called him Uncle Bum; I don't know,
maybe that's how we translated "brother."
I never knew his real name 'til I was grown
but I always remember the keys he pretended were the knife
he would use to cut off my thumb if he caught me sucking it.

Back then I liked the news more than even *The Twilight Zone*,
would run home from school just to hear Alec Gifford

and to watch Barnabas Collins on *Dark Shadows*.
It was my favorite program on T.V.
I'm glad our television was black and white then
'cause I don't think I could have watched
if I had seen the blood.
You know, I still like old vampire movies.

Butter beans were my favorite food.
And red beans, and ham hocks, and turkey necks
in brown gravy, and gumbo, and white rice with butter,
and bread pudding and, and … I don't know. I guess all of them,
but most especially butter beans,
slightly scorched, with fat pigtails filling the pot.
You know how to make the best bread pudding?
With stale French bread and your bare hands.
Somehow, squishing soggy bread ain't as much fun as it used
    to be.

And goodness, Sunday dinners were the absolute favorite!
We always ate early—about two o'clock—
roast, spiced with cloves and garlic,
oven-basted until it simmered in its own juices.
Macaroni, fat fat macaroni,
the kind I couldn't find when I moved to California.
baked in the oven with cheese all over the top
that turned crisp and brown around the edges
and peas that exploded in the pot.
Cornbread, crisp-edged, golden, slightly sweet
and smooth yellow potato salad
like they ain't even heard of in California.
No pickled hot dog relish here.

Uhm, Sunday dinner was sure good!
The best thing about Sunday dinner was dessert,
peaches and cream. You know, canned peaches in thick juice
chilled in the can overnight and then flavored with cream.
Okay, evaporated milk. I learned that phrase in California
after searching up and down a dozen store aisles
and trying to explain to half a dozen people what cream was.
We always ate Sunday dinner twice.
Momma expected it after feeding us so early
and then letting us run around outside all afternoon.

And I remember days when my mother made *lost* bread,
flour and water baked in the oven
then smothered with butter and strawberry jam.
Nothing like it for dipping in a good cup of coffee.

The first beginning I remember
is one where my mother's bed was in the front room
and me and my brother slept in the kitchen.
It must have been a dream
when I thought my mother tied him down to the bed
and said the boogie man was going to get him
if he didn't keep still.
She wanted him to rest
because he'd had an operation for a hernia.
We used to eat in my mother's room,
creamed corn and rice with smoked sausage.
Maybe I was two but who remembers
things from when they were two?

I don't know when it was I got that little egg shell baby.
I think we still stayed in the same place.
It was a tiny beige baby in its own blue blanket.
I loved it and my brother broke it.

In the other beginning—
at least the beginning I can recall with the most clarity—
we lived in the Seventh Ward, corner of Kerlerec and Marais,
shotgun house, huge fan, tiny bathroom window—
actually, the bathroom was outside.
I didn't understand that until years later
when I thought about walking barefoot across linoleum,
unlocking the back porch door, and stepping onto icy cement
surrounded by paper-thin walls.

Another beginning I remember is in a place I no longer know.
We stayed behind a lady who owned a huge pecan tree.
Her big sons would climb that tree when the pecans were ripe
and shake it 'til the yard disappeared under a brown blanket.
We could have all we wanted and we wanted a lot.
Wouldn't you if your grandmother made the best pecan candy
    in the world?

I'm not sure now if that's the same beginning
as the one when I was punished
for scuffing my new Easter shoes,
black patent leather lady shoes with colored patches at the tip.
I couldn't help it; our yard was really a bed of shells
and just walking on 'em scuffed your shoes.
Anyway, that year I had to stay on the back porch
and while I was standing there a girl came outside

from the house across the fence
we made friends and shared Easter eggs
so I guess it wasn't that bad after all.

When they weren't breaking things,
my brothers—three of them—and I
used to climb out the bathroom window and into the backyard.
Momma wasn't home but that wasn't why; we just liked to do it.
It was a small window and for us, quite a drop to the ground.
Or, we'd fall to pieces watching cleaners' plastic get sucked
through our huge kitchen fan and be spit out into the yard.
We'd climb through the bathroom window to get it
so we could do it again.
Naturally, my second brother did something dumb.
He threw the plastic pink baby spoon through the fan.
We didn't find it until months later
when our neighbors cut their grass.

On Marais Street I had another doll,
a beautiful chocolate brown baby
with black shoes, white baby socks,
a black and white dress trimmed in red ribbon
and a note that said, "Hold my hand, I'll walk with you."
Momma said Uncle DeDe and Aunt Billie brought it.
They came to find us after she and my daddy split.
And you know what? They were famous musicians.
I loved that doll. She even won first place in a baby doll contest.
My brothers broke that, too, and my glass dishes,
a tiny tea set we used for drinking red creme soda
and eating homemade pound cake.

My first Barbie doll won a contest, too,
only I lost her ribbon on the way home.
All those people on the bus
and one tiny straight pin to hold it on.
She was gorgeous in her three-colored hat and dress
with a white cancan slip underneath.
My mother had crocheted the whole thing except the slip.
She sewed that. My mother could do things like that.
They didn't have patterns for crocheted Barbie dresses
so my mother created her own, crocheting and ripping,
crocheting and ripping until she was able to adjust the bodice
for the oversized breasts, tiny waist, and wide hips.
Yeah, I know that doll didn't look nothing like me
but it was the most expensive toy I ever owned.

I was eight that Christmas and I got a sewing machine, too.
It was cast iron, red, with a wooden base that I decorated
with a yellow submarine sticker.
You could sew by winding the handle or using the batteries.
The first thing I made for my doll was a pleated skirt
from a scrap of plaid turquoise with golden stripes.
I did it without a pattern. You know I was proud.
Momma made clothes that way so I guess I got it natural.
I gave the machine to my first baby sister
when I left home after graduation.
She broke it. Seems people were always breaking my things.
I still have the doll. She's packed away somewhere.
Her straight hair probably untied, showing her bald scalp.

The spring of my second grade year I made my first communion,
a sort of Catholic Rite of Passage, I guess.

I don't remember because I'm not Catholic anymore
and anyhow in them days religion was tradition.
You were whatever your parents were. Period.
I was all dressed up in my white ruffled eyelet dress, cancan slip,
silky ankle socks with lace on the cuffs,
white buckle up patent leathers, Shirley Temple curls
that bounced with every turn of my head,
dainty white cotton gloves,
and a small white satin purse with a drawstring.
I was feeling pretty. I was the special one that day
and my heart was swelling. It nearly burst
when our neighbor and my mother's best friend, Miss Ruth,
gave me two shiny silver quarters—a whole fifty cents!
You can bet I pranced around all day, jingling those two coins,
sitting all prim and ladylike,
drinking with my pinky finger extended.
Every time I think of it I feel all bubbly inside,
like that Easter song we sang every year.
You know the one, "In your Easter bonnet,
with all the frills upon it,
You'll be the grandest lady in the Easter Parade."
You can bet my mom and her are still best friends
and you can sure bet she is still Miss Ruth to me.

The next summer I got the mumps.
I didn't know what it was. I mean, I was only nine.
All I knew was my throat hurt so bad
I couldn't swallow my cookies and milk,
the ones they give you when you go to those
summer enrichment programs at school.
Yeah, I know I was a strange child. I liked school.

Momma gave me that yucky cod liver oil
and even rubbed it all over my neck.
I really missed my cookies and milk.

I remember my first real kiss from my first real love.
We stood on rocks banking the Mississippi
at the edge of the Quarter.
They hadn't dressed it up then.
It was just a naked river, surrounded by rocks.
It was April, the sun was setting
and the world stopped when he kissed me.
That memory is as sweet now as the kiss was then.

In the end we stayed in the Desire Projects.
I learned to stay inside then,
except on summer Saturday afternoons
when we stuffed ourselves with watermelon
ice cold watermelon, sweet, so sweet, with salt sprinkled on top.
Every once in a while I hear myself chanting,
"Watermelon, watermelon, red to the rind."
We buried the seeds in our community yard, hoping
to grow our own watermelon so we could have it all the time.
We didn't call it a community yard
but with so many families stacked in together
and no fences to mark off what was ours, that's what it was.

We played tag in the grass there.
Trampled our watermelon sprouts running from the steel T's
of the clotheslines to the porch and back.
And we still climbed things:
the iron porch railings whose paint chipped off

in our rough grasp, the steel clothesline T's,
out the second floor hallway balcony window to the porch top.
We didn't jump from there though.
Momma would've killed us if we'd have hurt ourselves.

I spent more than half my life in the Projects
and remember so well how I wanted to escape.
It was a dirty, smelly, angry place.
The stench of roaches, garbage, and poverty
was more than I could bear.
The palm trees and desert sands of California
looked like heaven in comparison,
but California wasn't home.
They didn't know what cream was.
They didn't sell fat macaroni.
They couldn't even say chicory.

People thought I was crazy. I drove almost 2,000 miles,
practically nonstop, to get back to New Orleans
and knew when I hit the edge of the state
that I was home—by the scent of the air.
It smelled green, wet and green, humid, moist.
The only thing that smelled better
was my mother's coffee, with chicory,
that we dipped lost bread in the first night I was home
and we stayed up all night talking.

Sha'Condria Sibley
No Invitation to the Cookout

I.

As reward for being a self-proclaimed *ally*, an eager invitation
to the proverbial Blk cookout is given, and all of a sudden, I
lose my appetite. Am nauseous even. And I am not sure if it is
the thought of raisins in the potato salad or the sore sight of
bland bodies backing it up to a beat that exists only in their
own heads. All's I know is that when those who ain't *really*
family come to the party, the culture is never quite the same
or, in most cases, never seen again. That family will leave with
plates wrapped in foil, full of leftovers. While those who come
simply for a good time will stay and take the backyard *and* the
whole house with all your grandmama's recipes still trapped
inside. Their bellies full of food that they can't even digest
while the life of the party is left as bloated bodies.

II.

I pick up a used heroin needle to discard it before one of
Ms. Odessa's grandbabies gets a hold of it when a Ronald
Reagan doppelganger jogs by right in front of me, chest full
of conquest, smile sharp as syringe and as wide and as weapon
as the war on crack or on Blks. And all's I know is that when
those who plan on owning it come to the neighborhood, those
who gave it its name are the ones left running. That the drug
needles are never seen again. But neither are the Blk people.

Under the illusion that she is Blk woman's best friend, an *ally* walking her dog raises her paw to wave. And my sixth sense reminds me that I see dead people. That I see the ghosts of all who have died right there in the exact spot where her shitzu stops to mark both its own territory as well as its owner's. And I do not wave back. I do not make my body an American flag, welcoming illegal *white* immigrants only. Instead, I keep my cool and remain cold as I.C.E., trying my best not to melt under the heat of all the newest and hottest airbnbs that have now made tourist destination of a block that, according to Wayne, was once even hotter. Because all's I know is that when Subarus and Priuses with Connecticut and Colorado license plates come to the hood, the hood becomes a compact car with only enough room for those who were merely passing through to ride.

III.

And some will tell us to go back to Africa. But will turn around and follow us every damn where we go. Back to Africa. To the projects. To the hood. To the cookout. Will spread mayonnaise all over everything and call it a feast. Will hang *"We Buy Houses Cash!"* signs on everything and call your mama's house their new home in N'awlins. In Brooklyn. In Atlanta. In Baltimore. In _____.

All's I know is that none of this is random at all. That they have been crashing parties since *before* the first hood was ever created.

All's I know is that when those who ain't really family at all show up to wherever in the hell we are, we do not have to be gracious hosts, remembering that there are entire neighborhoods, cities, even continents full of reasons why they were never invited to begin with.

Sunni Patterson

My City Ain't for Sale

(Junebug Homecoming Project)

not my potions or my spells
not my crawfish or my crabs
not my brass or my ass
ain't none of it fa sale

not my cemetery or my temple
not my land or my love
not my "plareens" or my "huckabucks"
ain't none of it fa sale

you peeping toms and sallies
you wisconsins and nebraskas
you thieves and tax collectors
ain't nuthin ova here fa sale

not my theater or my park
not my music or my art
not my soul or my heart
ain't none of it fa sale

you bandits and you con men
you dumpster divers and hoodlums
keep your eyes off my prize
cuz ain't nuthin ova here fa sale

not my shotgun or my cottage
not my bar rooms
none of my houses
if you ain't hear it in the last announcement:
AIN'T NUTTIN OVA HERE FA SALE

not my Parrain or my Na'nan
not my "Aintee" or my Granny
my Paw-Paw
not none 'ah my family

I'm tellin ya
ain't nuttin ah' mine fa sale

not my sinners or my saints
not my coulds
not even my can'ts
don't see the picture?
lemme grab my paint
make it pretty, pretty use proper language:
There is nothing over here for sale!

not my culture or my crown
this city has had enough of you clowns
wanna build it up
but keep me down
oh, anything to make that sale?!
you want me to give you all I got
you want my window and my pot
Lawd knows it ain't a lot...
but its mine...
and it ain't fa sale

you don't know me or my kind
my heritage, my history, my line
my dignity, my legacy, my pride
some things just ain't up for buying
so while you gentrify and plot
while you calculate and allot
of all the things, put this one on top…

AIN'T NUTTIN OVA HERE FA SALE!

Skye Jackson

spoon-rest mammies

i.

on tuesday at work
my manager, a brown latina
married to a black man
approaches me

with a smile she sets
something down
in front of me
and asks
what do you think
about these?

i look down
at a porcelain spoon-rest
shaped into the swollen
figure of a mammy:

her lips exaggerated
& face dark
like the bark of a dead tree

the dress painted jemima red
with a white apron
tied chain-taut
around her waist

my heart races in its cage
after a second i say
we shouldn't sell these
they are offensive

my manager purses her lips
sighs and says
but they sell, my dear skye
people buy them

ii.

at the end of my shift
a latina woman
with frizzy bleached blonde
hair stands in front of me
she says
i'm from california
just buying these for my kids
as a joke

they're gonna be so mad
she says
they're gonna be so mad
i bought these

she hands me
two of the mammy spoon-rests
says
make sure you wrap them up good
i'd hate

for them to break
on the flight back home

so i protect them
in paper and bubble-wrap
carefully place each one
in a plastic bag
you know, the lady says
your store shouldn't carry these

i hand her the bag
smile and say
but they sell

iii.

three weeks later
my manager
hands me a cardboard box

i open it
to all the spoon-rest mammies
gathered together

they all smile up at me
from the guts of the box

my manager says
i tried to donate them to goodwill
but the guy accepting donations said:
i won't sell these

but if you want
i can throw them
in the dumpster out back

i'd be happy
to do that

Akilah Toney

Minstrel Jubilee 2019:
The New Orleans Negro

i have been commodified,
sold in the french market next to
voodoo dolls and lime hand grenades,
my body forces a rotting smile,
and i second line,
and i second line,
and i second line,
till blister bubbles form on the heels of feet,
my hips swaying in the stiff humidity,
my smile makes sharp cuts into my brown cheeks,
and colorful beads harness my neck like an iridescent noose,

my pain arouses white onlookers,
they clap with such joy and praise but i know,
their eyes say "dance nigga, dance!"
and i dance,
while time slows to mock me,
only speeding when i rest my body,
from the minstrelsy.

But after all is done,

I arise from the still warm ashes

More beautiful than ever...

Arthur Pfister aka Professor ARTURO
Wednesday, July 23, 2014, 3:38 AM, Stamford, CT

I'm So New Orleans...

(to Nadir Lasana Bomani and Byron Cole)

I'm so New Orleans I was born in Charity Hospital (on Mardi
  Gras Day)
I'm so New Orleans I hung out in the same bars as my teachers
  when I was 15-16 years old
I'm so New Orleans I know what's meant by Bulldogs, Rams,
  Green Hornets, and Purple Knights
I'm so New Orleans I still use HAI KARATE
  I use words like "BOO-COO BIG" and pronounce "Vieux Carre"
    as "*Voo* Carre"
  I'm so New Orleans I use words like "cornder" and I call
    anthrax "AMTRAK"
  I'm so New Orleans I say things like "ba-a-a-a-a-a-a-
    bay"...
  I know how to pronounce "Toulouse" and "Tchoupitoulas"
    (even though I cain't spell it)
I'm so New Orleans I have a framed pitcha of a chineyball tree
I'm so New Orleans I had a chineyball tree in my back yard
  on Dumaine St.
I'm so New Orleans I fell out a chineyball tree and broke my arm...
I'm so New Orleans I use any excuse to have a party (National New
  Orleans Day)
  I got Mardi Gras beads on my bedposts, wear orange,
    purple, green, and gold pajamas (and dream 'bout the
      Sixth Ward all night long)

I'm so New Orleans when I hear the name "Doctor" I know
    they ain't nobody sick
I'm so New Orleans when I hear the name "Professor" I know
    they ain't talkin' 'bout college
I'm so New Orleans when I hear "Hey, ba-a-a-a-aby" I *know*
    what they talkin' 'bout
I'm so New Orleans I know somebody named Trazi
    I know somebody named Afro
    I know somebody named Chopsley
    I know somebody named Zebadee and Oatie P.
    I know somebody named Blink
    I know somebody named Pink
I'm so New Orleans I know somebody named Stink...
I'm so New Orleans Father Grant told me, "Go to Clark, Champ,"
    where I had a track coach named Bacchus and a English teacher
        named Sanchez
I'm so New Orleans I read poetry at Borsodi's and The
    Neighborhood Gallery
I'm so New Orleans I call my tenth floor balcony "the gallerie"
I'm so New Orleans I know what it mean when a woman put
    dat red gravy on a man
    I know what it mean when a woman put salt in a man' shoes
        and I know what it mean when somebody burn a
            candle on you
I'm so New Orleans Bust Down is my favorite rapper
I'm so New Orleans I was watchin' the news about the civil war
    in Angola and thought it was about the jail
I'm so New Orleans my boy just got *back* from Angola (and I ain't
    talkin' 'bout Africa)
I'm so New Orleans I know the difference between Big Oil and
    Big Earl

I'm so New Orleans I remember when there was a black side
and a white side of the lake
I'm so New Orleans I remember Hap Glaudi makin' dat
statement 'bout "dat lil' monkey" (Never forget)
I remember when they dragged Avery Alexander down the
steps of City Hall (Never forget)
I lived through segregation and gentrification (Never forget)
I'm so New Orleans I can tell who be passin' cuz half my
family "bright" and half my family "dark"
I still grow plants (legal ones) in CDM cans and I cain't stand
canned gumbo, canned music, or canned red beans
I'm so New Orleans almost everybody I know cook, play music,
write poetry, dance, or drink me under the table
I'm so New Orleans I ain't gon' talk 'bout yo' daddy—I'ma
talk 'bout yo' momma
I'm so New Orleans when I'm back East I still say "trumpeTI-
ER" (insteada "trumpeter")
I call turtle "cowann" and I know dat "Kermit" is *mo'* than a frog...

I'm so New Orleans I used to wait for the bell peppers to go
on sale at Circle Food Sto'
I'm so New Orleans dat when I saw my uncle' pretty
girlfriend I thought she was a movie star
I still try to hold dat note on RAINBOW '65 and lose my
breath and start coughin'
I still look for Ban Lon shirts in the GOODWILL Sto' and I
still like day-old doughnuts rather than the fresh ones...
I had a pair of PF Flyers and upgraded to U.S. Keds
I rode the Sunset Limited all the way to California and oohed
and ah-ah-'d when relatives drove us to see Nat King Cole's
house

I'm so New Orleans my daddy told me he was gon' turn me
in to the gown men for a sack o' potatoes and 5 pounds o'
sugar…

I'm so New Orleans I play The Backatown Blues at my birthday
parties
I'm so New Orleans Mem Shannon is my favorite guitar player
(and cab driver), Willie Cole is my favorite drummer, and I
know Who Shot the La-La and Who Killa da
Chief…
I'm so New Orleans I climbed trees to get mispoleeves
I'm so New Orleans I live in Connecticut and have gumbo on
Sunday, red beans on Monday, seafood on Friday, and butter
beans on Saturday
I'm so New Orleans I know a former Bally Boy
I'm so New Orleans I got a BIG, BLACK umbrella
I'm so New Orleans I know 'bout the voodoo lady, the snow-
ball man, the knife-sharpening man, the milk man, the ice man,
the rag man, the feed man (who sold chickenfeed for
chickenfeed), the waffle man, the egg man, the cotton
candy man, the shrimp man, the paper man, and the
vejitibble man—"I got ba-*na*-nas, watermell-on, sweet
pat*o-oo-oo*-oo-oo-tee! I got ba-*na*-nas, watermell-on rade
to dee rind!—so goo-*oo-oo*—ood it keep the
ba-*a-a-a*-a-aby from cryin'!"

I'm so New Orleans I lived in a rented shotgun house and had
a garden in the back yard
I played with my army men in the back yard and me and my
daddy built a skatin' truck

I'm so New Orleans I saw swarming seas of mosquito hogs
    flyin' overhead on sweltering summer evenings back then
        (I don't know *where* they went)
I'm so New Orleans as a child I had a job on a softdrink truck
I'm so New Orleans all my momma' and daddy' friends
    became my aunts and uncles
I'm so New Orleans I took a $.25 ride and picture on a
    palomino pony in front my house
    I had a Hopalong Cassidy sweatshirt, a Fanner 50, and a
        hula-hoop
        (I ain't never played no jacks)
I'm so New Orleans I got a cousin named Zellie
I'm so New Orleans I have a cousin who was a Carnival king
I have a cousin workin' on her Ph.D. and a cousin who always
    inandouta jail…
I'm so New Orleans I went to visit somebody on the 3rd floor
    of Charity
    (and they wanted to keep me)
I'm so New Orleans people tell me, "Boy—you some crazy, yeah!"
I'm so New Orleans I remember shoppin' at Maison Blanche
    Annex
I'm so New Orleans my family took bus rides from the Sixth
    Ward to the lake for a picnic
I'm so New Orleans I remember standin' in front the window
    of Maison Blanche on Canal St. and staring at Mr. Bingle
I'm so New Orleans I always wondered why Mr. Bingle wasn't
    with Santy Claus on Christmas Eve
I'm so New Orleans I remember catchin' the City Park or the
    St. Bernard bus on the side o' KRAUSS
I'm so New Orleans I still play Tonk, Spades, and Pitty-Pat
    (for a quarter)

I still crush ice by wrappin' it in a white towel and
    bammin' it on the kitchen counter
I still wear tailor-made pants and wing-tipped shoes
I go to the repast when I don't even know the deceased
I make groceries and draw water
I went to the show at the Carver and the CLABON
    (in the same day) and I learned about sex at the
    X-rated theater on Canal St.
I'm so New Orleans I feel safe on Claiborne & Dumaine
I'm so New Orleans I remember when Edwin Edwards visited
    the 9th Ward
I'm so New Orleans I lined trashcans with the *States-Item* and
    the *Picayune*
I'm so New Orleans I saved money cuttin' grass, bought a
    TANDY Leathercraft kit, and made a leather belt and wallet
I'm so New Orleans I played BINGO at the church every
    week and I knew girls who dyed they hair with Kool-Aid...

I'm so New Orleans my momma worked for HASPELS and I
    had turtles and parakeets for pets
I'm so New Orleans I crushed up the French bread when my
    momma made puddin'
    My momma made the sign-of-the-cross on the French
        bread befo' she cut it
    My momma made my first dashiki
    My momma said, "Whoever don't like it—lump it!"
    My momma said, "I done brought you here—and I'll
        take yo' behind away!"
I'm so New Orleans my momma told me to stop actin' like I
    was born in Mandeville...

I'm so New Orleans I had uncles who was porters at the PLAYBOY
Club
I wanted to grow up and be a oyster shucker and we kept a
hatchet upstairs so we could break through the roof in case
of a flood…

I'm so New Orleans I tell people I'ma holler at 'em
I know what "humbug" mean
I know what "mawfiddice" mean
I know what "It ain't my fault" mean
I know what "Git-the-funk-out-my-face" mean
I'm so New Orleans I believe dat anybody with a law degree is
qualified to run for public office
I'm so New Orleans I know what misrepresentation and
undereducation mean
I know what "privatization" mean
I know what "Teach for America" mean
I know what "wind vs. water" mean
I know what "infill vs. landfill" mean
I know what "gentrification" mean
I'm so New Orleans I know what "they don't want us here no mo'"
(if they ever did) mean
I'm so New Orleans I announce dat I'm 'bout to do something…
"I'm fittin' to walk out the do'"
"I'm fittin'-nuh run to the sto'"
"I'm fittin'-nuh fry this fish"
"I'm fittin'-nuh berl these shrimps"
"I'm fittin'-nuh make these beans"
"I'm fittin'-nuh run to the washateria"
I'm so New Orleans I say, "I'm fittin'-nuh put these 13EEEs up yo'—
—LAWD TODAY!!!!!"

I'm so New Orleans I wrote a book called *My Name Is New Orleans*

I'm so New Orleans I get mountains of applause for my work—but molehills of purchases...

I'm so New Orleans I'm writing this long "I'm So New Orleans" poem

I'm so New Orleans I'm sittin' up here—half-sleep—writin' a poem 'bout how I'm so New Orleans...

I live on the East Coast and listen to WBOK every mornin'

If I see a bright-skinned dude up here I call him "Red"

I order setups in midtown Manhattan

I say, "Hey, baby" and rattle the radical feminists

I say Where y'at, yeah-ya-right, sho-ya'-right, I know DAT'S right and WHO DAT at poetry readings in Boston

I call the traffic island in New York "the neutral ground"

I was in Maine last week and was so excited 'bout seein' a mosquito hog I took a pitcha of it...

I'm so New Orleans I shopped at PAPS

I'm so New Orleans I used to wait for the bell peppers to go on sale at Circle Food Store

I'm so New Orleans I know a poet and college professor who grew up across the street from Hardin Park

I'm so New Orleans I put ketchup on grits, mynaze on lima beans, and potato salad on top my gumbo

I'm so New Orleans I eat erysters and I like gittin' crabs

I eat tails and suck heads (and say something like dat in public)

I'm so New Orleans I bought fried chicken from a bakery

I order SLAP YO' MOMMA online and I ask for yaca mein in Chinatown...

I'm so New Orleans a army general told me I wasn't a refugee—I was a displaced American

I'm so New Orleans I still drink rum & coke and all my
   girlfriends' mommas was barmaids
I'm so New Orleans my momma told me, "If you don't stop
   dat cryin'—I'ma give you something to cry *'bout!*"
I'm so New Orleans I been in Tony's Green Room, Joe and
   Jean's, Bazanac's, The House of Joy, Hank's, Blunt's, Mulé's,
      the Peacock, the Snowflake, Devil's Den, Dell's, the
         Brown Derby, the Blue Goose, Desert Sands, and
            the Cozy Corner (anywhere but
               Tuckey's Dome)
   I still make shrimp Po-boys on Fridays and ask for hot
      sausage sandwiches (in New Haven)
   I like to hear the scratches on the old records and I
      know what sport Isaiah King and Charlie Powell played
I'm so New Orleans I call A.P. Tureaud "London Ave." and I
   call Oretha Castle Haley "Dryades St."
   I *still* call the projects by they old names (even if they ain't
      'round no mo')
I'm so New Orleans I'ma mow my absentee neighbor's lawn
   and git they lot (You know you *wro-o-o-o-ong* for dat)

 I'm so New Orleans I been all over the U.S. and traveled abroad
   (and still know there ain't nuthin' like a Sixth Ward woman)
 I like big lips, big hips, and big tips (I'm a waiter)
 I'm so New Orleans I live on the East Coast—with all these
   fine, rich, smart, pretty wimmins—and cain't stop thinkin'
   'bout dat BIG, FINE woman in the 9th Ward…

I'm so New Orleans…
   I get tongue-tied when I try to pronounce the word
      "gentrification"

-when I try to pronounce the word "asphyxiation"

-when I try to pronounce the word "consciousness"

-when I try to pronounce the word "hypothesis"

-when I try to pronounce the word "innuendo"

-when I try to pronounce the word "subliminally"

-when I try to pronounce the word "abominable"

-when I try to pronounce the word "antithesis"

I'm so New Orleans I get tongue-tied when I try to
    pronounce my own last name...

I'm so New Orleans I bought plants and 45 RPMs in the
    backa KRESS

I'm so New Orleans I call marbles "chinees" and I call subway
    tokens "carfare"

    I got a friend named Dago (and he ain't Italian)

I'm so New Orleans I know a straight man named DeCuir

    I know a dark-skinned dude named Snow

    I got a black friend named Whitey

    I got a white friend named Craig X

        —and I still make the sign-of-the-cross whenever I
            pass a church

I'm so New Orleans people away from home think I speak a
    foreign language

I'm so New Orleans I obliterate the language

I'm so New Orleans insteada sayin' "Excuse me" I say "Oops, my
    ba-a-a-a-a-ad"

I use words like "bammin'"

I use words like "cornder"

I say things like "ba-a-a-a-a-a-*bay*"...

I ask for sammiches "dressed" and order pepper sausage and liver
    cheese at New York delis...

I say things like "I like-ted dat"

I say things like "LAWD, HAIR MERCY!!!!"

I say things like "You ain't never lied"

I ask people, "Ya' *heard* me?!!" (when I know good & well they did)

I start sentences off with "Back in the day..." and end 'em with the word "yeah," *yeah*...

I'm so New Orleans I use the word "some" as an adjective

I say things like "Dat's some nice, yeah"

I tells wimmins, "You some pretty. You some pretty, yeah... You pretty from teef to toe"

I'm so New Orleans I say: "*Gir-r-r-r-r-rlll*—you some fine, yeah!"

I'm so New Orleans I say: "*Uhm-uhm-mmmm*...Dis some good, yeah!"

I'm so New Orleans Facebook's translator pop up when I write something...

I'm so New Orleans I carry a umbrella under live oak trees so I don't get stung by caterpillars

I'm so New Orleans my sister worked for the racetrack

I'm so New Orleans I worked for SUNO, the Job Corps, and the Urban League

I'm so New Orleans my name is Arthur, but my nickname is Billy (?????)

I'm so New Orleans I refer to the elders by a "Mr." or "Miss" befo' they FIRST— rather than they last—name

I'm so New Orleans I called my grandmother "Mah-Dear"

I got people in my family named Doona, Doody, Boobie, Junior, Pah-DEE, and Tee-TEE

I know people named Mah-DOO, Boo, Zigaboo, Black Boo, Cayou, Bubby, Nubby, Bay-*BAY*, Ray-*Ray*, Too-*Too*, Mah-*Moo*, Bob-*Boo*, Noo-*Noo*, Bob-*Bee*, and Schneckenburger...

I know cats named Big Wooty, Lil' Wooty, Noony, Doony,
Dip, Big Harold, Lil' Harold, Big George, Lil' George,
Big Herman, Lil' Herman, Big Hicky, Lil' Hicky, and
a lady named Big Willie...
I got friends named Pissy and Pissy-Boo and three friends
named Country
I got friends named BIG ED and friends named Lil' Bit and
Piece O' Me (his momma named him dat)
I got BIG, FAT FRIENDS and lil' itty-bitty skinny friends (and
I luvv 'em *all*)
I know somebody named Soraparu, Hookfin,
Cockerham, Dooky, and Pasooky
I even know a woman named Nooky (and she *like* to be
called dat)
I know people named Red, Black, Brown, and Blue
I'm so New Orleans I ran into UptownzIllest in a record store
on Canal St. and I know Ricardo "Big Easy" Wilson
I know a woman named Keion and a brother named Mandingo
I'm po'—but I'm on a first-name basis with the bank
president...
I had high school classmates named Willoughby, Woodfork,
and Woodfox
I had high school classmates named Smitty and Kitty
I'm so New Orleans I had a high school classmate named...
Titty
I'm so New Orleans I played baseball for the Gentilly
Warriors and thought people who lived in Pontchartrain
Park was rich
I'm so New Orleans my gran'ma, my momma, my sisters, my
cousins, and my aunts wore Daniel Green slippers (some
still wear 'em, but they ain't gon' tell you dat)

I remember when Christian Unity Baptist Church was a
  bowling alley and I laugh when I hear the words **"LET HER
  HAVE IT"**
I'm so New Orleans I ate at Chez Helene's on Robertson after
  my high school prom and went to weddings in the Lafitte
  Project
I know 'bout the lady who grazed her horse on the levee
  and I learnt how to swim in Lake Pontchartrain
In fact—I pronounce Pontchartrain *"Punch*atrain"
I'm so New Orleans I know 'bout the big, round pool in Abita
  Springs and went to Boy Scout camp in Indian Village
I still play Joe Tex records and I can hear the music, smell the
  roux, and feel the love…
I'm so New Orleans I sense both the magnificence and
  longsuffering of the people
I'm so New Orleans that I sing and shout and holler their praises
  their beauteous splendor that inspires and amazes
  their colors and smells and street vendor yells…
I'm so New Orleans I surrender to its splendor
  and rejoice in its beatific bosom
I'm so New Orleans every word and deed I attempt to portray
  in my poetry was,
    is, and will be about the city that blossoms in my heart
      like a flower and springs from
        my fingers like tongues of fire…

I'm just so New Orleans…

Mona Lisa Saloy

New Orleans,
a Neighborhood Nation

Possums sleep, middle of the road sometimes, invade soggy
   walls after hurricanes dump heavy rains, hide in clothes
   closets and eat through my canvas book bags, must taste
   like peanut butter and strawberry jam, the pages of
   wisdom spread like confetti on the floor.

10,000 spiders live in my neighborhood. What grows wild
   sticks like thorns. What crawls will bite you red and blue.
   Roaches spread wings past dusk, invade doorjambs. We
   grow, eat, and love okra; there

Ain't no proper gravy without a little slime. Veggie slimes are
   us Black folks on this planet.

We know folks backwards and forwards, translate: to every
   little thing, nothing forgotten.

Y'all is singular, plural, and a sweet sound in our ears.

Festivals are us: shrimp, satsumas, tomato, rice, crawfish,
   blues & jazz.

We throw hissy fits in a heartbeat. Find cayenne, salt, onion,
   celery, parsley, and thyme on yardbirds baked, fried, or
   stewed, even on the other white meat, anything that swims
   in a bayou, lake, mud, or river: Catfish, grouper, red fish,
   crab, sheephead, *Cawain.*

Out of bread? Whip up *gallait* (pan-fried shortening bread) or
fritters deep-fried with ripe bananas or a pocket of plantains in
season; just honey to taste.

When weather dips below 70, not too low, our winters without
cold, then it's gumbo time. Okra, seafood, or beans *de jour*: red
beans, white beans, butter beans, crowder peas

Plus black-eyed peas, the eyes of God on us.

We still make hucklebucks in summer. Make suppers to raise
bucks for folks stuck between a Rock & a hard place, and pass
potato salad over a fence for a backyard barbeque with hot beer
and Hurricane cocktails at sunset in yards, or on galleries glad
for time measured in minutes.

Maurice M. Martinez

Niggers I Have Known

an excerpt from *Blackcreole:*
Too White to be Black, Too Black to be White

[…] "So today you're a poet?" I asked.

"Yeah, I've been reading Langston Hughes. That cat's where it's at. Like the one poem he wrote called, 'I Have Known Rivers.'"

"I know the poem. It's very nostalgic, very deep!"

Hongry reached again into the box crate on his skatenin' truck and pulled out a spiral notebook. "I wrote a poem like that las' Sadday," said Hongry. "I call it, 'Niggers I Have Known.'"

"Some people would find that title insulting," I replied, "especially Black people."

"Go haid, there you go again, tryin' to erase Nigger reality with Negro-ology. Context, man. It's all in the context," exclaimed Hongry.

"What do you mean by context?" I asked.

"Feelings, it's how you feel when you say a word. I call it '*myfeelings*' context. Some words bring with them a positive feeling, like for example: beautiful, groovy, choice, wonderful. Thems nice words. Other words bring a bad feeling wif 'em: stupid, dumb, ugly, fucked up. Thems negative words. An' still other words are neither complimentary or negative: innocent, naïve, out of it, dreamy, air head, harmless. Thems neutral words."

"Yes," I replied. "I remember hearing a lecture by linguist Ken Johnson who said the same thing, that words may have a psychological meaning that is positive, negative, or neutral."

"But now, we got some words that have all three '*myfeelings*' wrapped all into one. Like the word 'Nigger,'" said Hongry. "Nigger can be positive, negative, and neutral. Like for example, negative: 'Nigger, you better git outa my face!' 'Oh George,' cried the white housewife, 'you've got to do something. The Niggers is taking over!' 'Go sit in the back, Nigger!' Thems offensive uses. Then there's a neutral use: 'Aw, you see that Nigger over there? Don't worry about him, he ain't shit.' And then there's the positive use of the word Nigger: When two Black males meet, one says, 'Hey, ma Nigga! You lookin' good!' in a laughing tone to compliment another person. And it can also mean love. Like about 2 am in the morning when she looks up at you and sighs, 'Oohhhhh my sweet n i g g e r.' So you see, Nigger can have all three of '*myfeelings*,' depending on the context. But white people better never use it 'cause they done abused it so much in the past that it hurts."

"Yeah, you right!" I exclaimed.

"It's in the blood. Mother Africa. That's why I decided to write a poem. I call it:

"NIGGERS I HAVE KNOWN," replied Hongry. "It goes like this:

I have known niggers,
Good niggers, bad niggers,
Half-ass CPT (Colored People Time) niggers,
Slick niggers,
Smart niggers,
Hard-working niggers.
Talkin' niggers,
I once knew a nigger (a high school principal)
Who could out-nigger
Any nigga.

I have known niggers,
ASSimilated beyond repair house niggers:
Quiet Never-say-nuthin'-always-votin'-against-us
Supreme Court Uncle Tom Clarence-the-Silent-Sam
    Turncoat nigger,
And Militaristic-Conformist-Collegespeak Condoleezza,

Utah un-black married-white Haitian Mormon conservative
    woman politician
Wanna-be Republican tight-ass suit-n-tie niggers, like
    Sleepy Medicineman Uncle Ben,
Who believes that kidnapped Africans in the bottom of
    slave ships were immigrants,
And Poverty is a state of mind…Brainlessman Benny, made
    big bucks carvin' in yo' haid,
sittin' n' grinnin' on TV, trumped-out in Prez-Agent-
    Orange-the-pussygrabber's face.

I have known negative niggers wallowing in cesspools of
    their own petard,
Tryin' real hard to escape the everyday pains of being unhappy
By blaming, like a dog that bites the hand that feeds him,
    blaming & biting.

Pompous know-it-all-done-it-all Boo-gee
    sippin'-in-suburbia Sugarhill niggers.
Big Chump You-Ain't-Nuthin'-But-A-Popcorn niggers,
Black-skin-white-lame-brain-sell-out pan-handlin'
    git-nin'-over Anglo-Saxon niggers
Niggers who forgot they wuz once Niggers,
Nigga please!

Hustling New York Harlem-to-Bed-Stuy squinchy-eyed
    niggers,
Mohn-fah-die Jinney-woman *Ma-Gwa* (Big Mouth) niggers
Fulla *Mashuquette* (gossip), love to tell yo' bizness all over
    town.

Housing Project Chicago niggers,
Assembly line Detroit niggers,
Dope haid niggers, urban gun-toting dope-dealing
    Gangstas who shoot to kill.
California Cockhounds who love to make love, kiss-bliss
    transplanted from Onzaga St.
Jiveass Graham Cracker Niggas who don't know they ass
    from a hole inna' ground.
An' Uganda niggers you try to help all yo' life, givin' them
    gigs and money
For 50 years, and who out-of-the-blue one day, tappin' on
    a conga,
Turn on you like a cornered hungry rat, blaming you for
    them being in poverty;
Bitter, pre-dementia envy,
Crying in sad baby-pouts, "You ain't never done shit for me!"

I have also known
Nice niggers, positive niggers, sharing-caring niggas,
niggers who would give you the shirt
Off they back.
An' some Oreo Dipshit niggers who don't want
To be Black.
Ca-Goo (Touched-in-the-head, not-playing-with-a-full-deck,
    crazyass) Niggers.

I have known niggers,
Fun-loving niggers
niggers who could out dance, out step,
Out dress, out sing, out rap anybody
Talented niggers
niggers who could play
Anything musical.
niggers who got soul.

I have known niggers
With insights, Common sense niggers,
Entrepreneurial niggers, cool in the pool of corporate survival.
Thinking niggers, investment money-making niggers,
Intellectual niggers, artists, poets and Sun-Ra expressionists,
Articulate spoken-word leaders, doctors & surgeons, lawyers,
TV Newscasters, savvy media spokespersons,
Politically successful niggers,
Compassionate niggers,
Niggers who could fix
Whatever got broke,
And Hypertension Worry-All-la-Time-Texting Facebook niggers
    Who died from a stroke....ONLINE.

I have known a lot of niggers North South East and West,
But there ain't no nigger
Like a New Orleans hot sausage raid-beans-n-rice nigger;
I know
He's the best.

I have known niggers
Big Niggers...Skinny niggers...Fat Stomach niggers

Hatchet-haid niggers
Stomp down niggers
Niggers both short and tall,
My soul has grown deep with nigga-Rhythms,
And I love them rhythms all.
Dig what Ah'm sayin', Stuffy Smiff, No Shit,
Put that in yo' acorn pipe and…smoke it!

But the worst nigger is the Non-Black
Blandass Bigot—praying under a steeple—
Who hates Black people
            —Hongry."

"Go haid on, *couzain* (cousin), that's a well-written poem. But you're going to have to say a Novena after writing that poem," I said.[…]

Akeem Martin

Sunsets

We use to watch sunsets for fun
Now
The sunset illuminates the gutting of the living room
My mother's house is my New Orleans

She must be emptied
all her children must leave
all the furniture must move out
the neighborhood won't have the same music as it use to
Gentrification will act as a anti depression cocktail
the bike lanes will mirror the veins along her arm

New Orleans lost her possessions for the third time today
Her foundations
look like tombstones
Her memory is her casket
"I grew up on that street
My Mom's house use to be around that corner"
written as her last words in the obituary
When she cries
the Street's flood
the gutters remember the taste of
History floating with waterlogged bodies in the Mississippi

Ayo Fayemi-Robinson

o.d.

we have overdosed on being wise
the road weary horde
heeding the call
cramped and crowded
in shelters, hotels and homes of hosts
who believed it would be just
a few days

we have overdosed on criticized
the overbaked rescued
stranded and starved
on interstates and in decimated halls
of unconventional unconcern

overdosed on ironic surprise
hearth guard hatchet bearers
ascending steps and attic
stares from the rooftops
of ruins, we braved it
all to protect, and there
is nothing left

we are overdosed on charitized
eating sentiment-seasoned
complementaries, needing
levees and elevation planes
insurance meant to recompense
and one last claim

for justice

I have known epidemics, vicissitudes, and calamities:

—Tar-barrels flaming at street-corners, and big guns

barking defiance to plague-stricken air...

Quo Vadis Gex-Breaux

Waterlogged,
Nomadic Katrina Songs

I

After two months in the washing machine
my softest pima cotton sheets
bought at a sale's sale
were mildew mottled.
Bleach was not enough
to clear the stains.
Refusing to throw them away
I continue to work on them
like we continue
to work on New Orleans
longing for its former comforts
aching for the familiar.

The uncity that remains—
pock-marked
filled with emptiness and darkness
isolated and isolating
is weeping
mourning its loss of joy
its people
its way of being.

Where do we bathe our feet?
Where do we anoint our heads?
Where do we quench our thirsts?

Wash our crud-filled fingernails?
How can we ever trust water,
our former friend, again?

II

Cypress trees were at home
in the head height water.
Oaks strove not to die.
Baseboards in houses buckled
water soaked and swollen
like the minds of the scattered
who left for just a couple of days
or the rescued who were herded
onto planes and buses to places
where gumbo is a foreign word
a phantom dish someone mentioned
when she was trying to sound exotic.
New homeless.

Random thoughts, destinations, emotions and anger
powerful enough to blow up another three levees
fill our heads, swell our hearts.
But with no place to go—full—
we roam the insides of our souls
the building-trash strewn streets of a town
sacrificed to the water gods
for the price of an engineer's early lunch.
We roam the places that we used to know
corner stores that served Friday shrimp and oyster
po-boys with bottled root beer, our Katrina-dead auntie's
drowned house, gutted coffee shops.

There is no sense to make of this
yet, it is so far from nonsense.
There is no place in our heads for the numbers
tolled and untolled dead
dead in the water
dead after the water
dead stuck to the living room floor
heartsick dead
fleeing dead—caught by the scythe on the run
dead spirits walking
dead alive looking for their
kin and kith—their kind
here, there and every where.

The dead roam ready to haunt
an already haunted city
for the rest of its natural and
unnatural days.

Whatever the personal level of loss
everything, house, car, electronics,
clothes, or nothing to not much—
We've all lost our home
the place that cradled our wanton ways
abided our idiosyncrasies,
supported our street characters and
fed us body and soul
the food of creativity and high spirits.

Shadows will not be innocuous here.
Man-made disaster breeds menacing spirits.

Angry shadows who know they were robbed
of time and offered unwillingly
on water altars to gods they never
dreamed of worshipping.
demand unquiet retribution.

Christopher Williams

These Men, New Orleans Men

Douglas Redd

Morris F.X. Jeff, Jr.

Jomo Kenyatta-Bean

Kojo Livingston

Baba Takuna Tarharkah

Babatunji Ahmed

Tom Dent

Harold Battiste

John Scott

These men, New Orleans men, pushed, championed and
    helped build the culture of this great city.

Fighters writers flame igniters

Horn players sooth sayers

Preachers and painters

Their work alone would have made them great

Even had they not been teachers mentors and father figures to
the little eyes watching their deliberate moves

Even had not those men taught what they learned

Even had not their legend spread like spirit fire

They would still be great.

Culture bearers are the professors of these big easy streets

Where art and heart meet

How function and purpose collide

The why and the what for and the who for and the when

No just because

Never for the hell of it

Even if we raise hell in the process

We cross roads and cross swords

Only cross words when necessary

Our cussin aint always fussin

We just gettin our point across

So when we fight **for real for real**

We keep the upper hand

Emotion is high and these old new Orleans spirits is always
lurkin round

Looking for a soul to ride for the night

And when we catch one

It usually come out as a song or a poem

Or a speech

Could be a sculpture or painting

A sermon or curse

Come thru so fast you cant reverse

A play or decree

Or could just be

A talk you havin with me

See these men, New Orleans men, lived what they did

Thought word action life

The process

They passed it on before they passed on

I see them everyday

I smell the paint

Hear the notes

Feel the rhythms

Read the quotes

Or words spoke

Or metal stroked

They lived what they did

Loved who they did it for

And for that

We honor them

Hold them up and speak their names

Ancestors

Never forgotten

Eternal life thru us

These men, New Orleans men, we give thanks and say

Asé

Ayo Fayemi-Robinson

Tribute to Carol Bebelle

(In celebration of decades of service as Executive Director of Efforts of Grace, Inc., and Ashé Cultural Arts Center and in expectation of more wonder yet to unfold)

Tonight, we pay homage to the source of everything.
We honor the sacred hidden spaces that nurture creation,
before there is clarity in the imagination.

We gather to give thanks for the birth and rebirth
of the possibility of making it real,
made palpable by the energy and vibration
of our visionary master of manifestation, Carol Bebelle.

The gallery for our installations,
a stage for our poems and plays,
the Mothership of our music and musings,
Carol is our phenomenon,
giving birth to generations of phenomena.

Carol is a queen in that cadre of elders
who are for us our standard bearers,
and what more formidable institution builder
than the one who tells us to focus not on what is,
but on what could be?

And what could be better than our Bebelle,
borne within the sacred hidden spaces
that nurture creation,

before there exists even an idea
of that something that wants existence?

We gather to give thanks for the birth and rebirth
of imaginings made possible, made palpable
by the energy and vibration of our Carol Bebelle.

We are with you to keep on shining and showing
what can be—what will be. So, come on Carol Bebelle;
keep on Carol Bebelle; run on Carol Bebelle;
keep on Carol, keep on!

Peteh Muhammad Haroon

City of My Birth

we are as diverse as Mothers
I'm talkin' 'bout from neo-griots
to Lady buck jumpers
from French Quarter musicians
to tap dancing magicians
high school bands
to Cats playing the Blues and Zydeco

And don't talk about that Black Man
With a' empty "Thunderbird" bottle and a stick in his hand
behind Big Chief
With no teeth in his mouth
Talkin' 'bout
"ain't I prrreeeettyyyyy"
Don't sleep on my cityyyy

Believe it or not, the 7th ward still got a couple of die hard
    Bally Boys
The whole city knows that Micey is a Muslim now, running
    with Farrakhan
But the whole city still hurt that Soulja Slim ain't make it out
    the game, he in the grave shot down

In New Orleans we got good reason to be like "fuck the music
    industry"
We rather music in the streets
Culture flows thru our veins
Our roots run deep

Our unique art and culture helps to ease our minds

That's why we be buckin' at second-lines… whoonah!

pretty pretty Spy Boy stay with it on his mind

pretty pretty Spy Boy stay with it on his mind

This place here is like the land of that fire-water

Where we dance to "do whatcha wanna"

Get full of that marijuana

And blow trumpets like Kermit Ruffins

This is a city where blue collar workers spend 2g's on a pair of
shoes just to go dance in the streets and scuff 'em

We call it tradition, people who don't understand call it
wasteful, ignorant and stubborn

People always talking about how New Orleans be coming

But down here family really means something

It really is a man's worth

Damn near everybody got an Aunt Pudding who be cooking
after church

Who be Looking past your sins and helping you clean off your
dirt

I'ma forever rep' the city of my birth!!

Kristina Kay Robinson

Indian Red

—my lover, my friend, my adversary.

I miss you on Sunday.
I look for you amongst the feathers, behind a mask
search this crowd for your face.

I said that I would not come out this year
that I have nothing to celebrate,
too many things to mourn.
Yet in still the downbeat lulls me
here.

New Orleans is a sea of ghosts.
Everywhere
are reminders of those things
beautiful and lost forever.

*Reveling in the quickening of Progress within and
around me, I sing of the bewildering expanses
of far-reaching bridges and overpasses...*

Michael "Quess?" Moore

comfort food

it's that moment in New Orleans traffic
when the stockpiled cars form blood clots in the city streets
when the whole damn small town is a congested body
overrun with clogged arteries
when you become the self-loathing mouth of this unhealthy
    body
cursing every moment that led you to a moment so stifled
looking for meaning in this madness
for a metaphor like a doctor's diagnosis
or perhaps the otoscope to shed light on the situation
when you remember how much fun it is stuffing your face
with more than you can handle in the first place
how much comfort you've always found in this town's food
no matter how bad the indigestion

G.F. Smith

A poem for New Orleanians in the Key of Hamlet Called "That Is the Question"

To New Orleans
or not to New Orleans

A question asked since long before 1803
By a big complex wrapped up in a little man
Planning a war in Shakespeare's land

And now in 2016
we find ourselves at the intersection of Napoleon…
and Claiborne

Staring down the double barrel of a streetcar track named…

Traffic.

Bumper to bumper
Standing still,
Wondering whether tis nobler to suffer in the mind, body, and
    will
or to take arms against a Mississippi river of troubles.

Ride out the storm…. Or evacuate

To leave
Or not to leave

New Orleans is your heartache and your happy place
separated by two city blocks
Therein lies the rub
marinated into your meat
Ain't no sleep!
Wake up to the burning sensation burping up whiskey
and the spicy dancing inside your chest of Boiled crawfish feet

Step into streets
Secondlining through the obstacle course of shell casings and
    chalk outlines

#ThomasRolfesrestinpeace

Weaving your way through orange caution cones
Dodging pothole after pothole
Only to find out today is Sinkhole de Mayo
City sinking in debt from the last regime
T.O.P.S. now closed cause of Bobby's holes.

To steal
Or not to steal

Politicians, policemen, and principals
Ignoring problems, seeking profit
Parish prison overflowing with citizens
caught in the Ponzi scheme called traffic court
Parish prisons overflowing with victims

Revolving door policies instead of trying harder
This rehab failed; let's try the other

Out goes one, in comes another
Am I still talking about the jail or am I talking about school
    charters?

Our lack of social conscience does make us all cowards at our
    core
Our laissez faire,
too big,
too easy to ignore
Our neighbors still gone, replaced by foreigners
putting their quietus on our music, making ordinance of our
    culture.
Gentrification swam in to wade in our waters
Perchance while we were sleeping in the land of what dreams
    may come
our homes have become Air BnB stores.

This is not time to dream
It's time not to dream.

New Orleans

 We are more than our Mardi Gras
We are not just our Jazzfest
We are better than Cardell Hayes' decision to follow
We are better than Will Smith's decision to leave the scene
We are not Gusman's orange clad slaves
We are not Uncle Piyush gutting our father while seeking to
    be king
We are not a storm surge
We are not our waterlines
We are not Katrina's above ground graves.

We are a half slave dance/half improvisation
    so simple but profound you can only have been born with it,
        that responds from the whole of your body
            when called by brass horns at a "Super Sunday."

We are the gentle roar of the St. Charles street car
    gliding through the "neutral ground"
        beneath a mane of Spanish moss,
            flowing from the crown of a majestic Oak.

We are humidity thick enough to pick from the air with your
    tongue, like bubbles,
        while standing on your Royal St. balcony
            twenty feet above ground
                dead even to sea-level

We are the bright light the world crowds around
    campfire style
        capillarity combusting from Canal and Bourbon's wick
            Bling Bling

We are all our sins remembered and all our songs forgotten.
We are New Orleans

So you must ask yourself this one question
Do you want New Orleans to be…
Or not to be?

Tom Dent

Return to English Turn

this
barren place on
river road english
turn
where river turn

this
cemetery small old wooden
crosses
weeds this spot
where Bienville convince english
this land lay french
sign say
1699

nothing but the woosh
of occasional strong
breeze
levee green
it
is
here
it all began

the french push
the people
who live here
out

go west young indian man
and come up this river turning
here
in droves pushing themselves up
over and over those years
at the bottom
groaning leaning straining to
the river current
us
the music of our ruptured memory
beat out by the music
of chains

plantation thrived
here
off the work of Leroy and
Beulah orange trees
great house
cotton and sugar
and chains

songs and shouts
the forgotten pains
the rebellion
and the hangings
at every parish church
above and below this
barren place

then the boats
up and down this
muddy snake with
the sugar and the cotton
and the corn
up and down
past this barren place
to France and England and
Cincinnati
Memphis
Chattanooga
Philadelphia
trying to bring this river under
machine control
commerce thrive
we work the boats
live in shacks by the new tracks
and look to the river
where will it bring us
what will it bring us

then
something went wrong
something went strange
something went weird
the plantation begin to slip away
the foundation

     begin to rock
     to the pulse
     a the rivuh

current oh muddy
rocking slipping straining
slipping rocking swinging
oh current oh
crazy muddy rivuh
what you doin
what you doin!
whas happenin
you done moved in
on us oh crazy rivuh
its de *moon*
de ju ju
crazy le bas
leavans be look down on dis
what is it in this night
everything fallin fallin
slipping away
floating down de
old crazy rivuh

bells/steeples/cotton mattresses
hoes/sickles/draywagons
China from Europe
rugs from Turkey
picture of painted faces
mirrors/columns/moss-covered oaks
stuck in the moon mud
chains/whips/flintlocks
cypress doorways/stained glass windows
thin iron fences/spiral staircases
stuck in the mud

stuck in the mud
and the river wouldn't stop

*   *   *   *   *

so see us now in the city
to the direct north
the crazy city the city
of de pleasure unpostponed
city of raindreams
of raindreams
moon-night mare city

city we built
tradesmen and mechanics and craftsmen
with Dahomey-honed crafts
city we carve from de swamp
and in tall plaster glass steel
building fortunes made and lost
but not ours
our music stolen made
circus show for drunk
whiskey dreams not ours
while straw-hatted newly
americaine rulers sweat
through dey sear-sucker suit
wipe brows over oyster
contemplate next move
we seethe in project heat
the glass broken the steel
jutting at us the plaster chipped

our streets mud
our whiskey dreams endless
our music drowns the rain
soothes the cuts from shards

we seethe in project heat
we seethe in memories
ship hull ship boiler
cane field weeded shack
city dock city factory
orange tree
brick over cemetery
forced river journeys
past this place
this barren spot
making the sharp turn
over and over and over

and now we look to the old craggy
river
we look for deliverance
as the spirit of our ancestors
hovers above this place harvesting memory
may our gods watch over the long journey
may our god of music
bestow grace on us
as we journey until the river
goes wrong again in the night

then may
centuries of building

on forced journeys
return to the silence
of this spot now
nothing but the woosh
of occasional strong   breeze
levee green
ship mast in the distance
where river
turn

Kalamu ya Salaam

Beneath the Bridge

(A 2006 eulogy for North Claiborne Avenue from
Canal Street down to Elysian Fields)

beneath the bridge on claiborne avenue, there,

where the mardi gras indians used to go
and offer up their colorful vows to never bow down
as they trodded around the mean streets of this sacred town
freely treating our eyeballs to the most prettiest,
feathered, multi-hued suits that any man
could ever hope to sew and wear in any given lifetime,
they hollered the chants of saints,
their eyes burning with the fire of the guardians
of the flame sounding out sacred syllables in a language without
name, words whose meanings we could not specify
but whose dynamic intentions none of us could deny;

where once tall oaks grew spreading magnificent branches
that embraced whole families of revelers joyfully enjoying
a home-cooked holiday brunch, iron horseshoes clanging
as poppa p threw a dead ringer and junior dug
a serving spoon into aunt juanita's mustard-colored
potato salad while ambrose sat with his latest girlfriend
    snuggling in his lap, lying through his gold-capped
teeth about how much money he won betting on the ponies
    last week and how he was paying for this whole spread
out of just a small portion of the purse he achieved
when he selected a horse whose number

was the same as this girlfriend's birth date
or was it the thirty-something double digit
that was both her bust and her butt tape measurement?;

where the concrete construction of a federal expressway
created a sound-box that high school bands rolled through
inter-threading the ebony thighs of teenage girls
with aural ribbons of raucous marching music played
with a buck-jump beat the song's composer never intended
or imagined, shouted out with an upful, youthful swagger
whose chocolate sweetness was so deep that all you could do
was smile, and smile as the parade provided
a sonic prescription for whatever ailed you;

where along either side of the street used to thrive
haberdasheries (which offered everything worth wearing,
from congressional sky pieces to tailored peg-legged pants dyed a
diversity of tints & shades selected from a rainbow
of pigments that made technicolor seem dull,
not to mention stacy adams shoes whose shine
was so gleaming you did not need a mirror);

where doctor's offices and pharmacies, grocery stores
and mortuaries, flower shoppes and butcher stalls
testified to the industriness of an urban community
still shaking country dust off its boots,
run right up next to passé-blanc dynasties
that had been resident in these homes
since the slavery time plaçages that produced
their pale-skinned lineages;

where houston's school of music was on one side
and the negro musicians' union was on the other,
and barbershops and hair salons hosted weekly
informal town hall meetings at which every manner
of contemporary problem was advised and analyzed
in betwixt the salacious shoo-shoo
of who did what to whom and why;

where a veritable smorgasbord of eateries
such as levatas seafood that specialized
in chilled half-shelf oysters deftly shucked
as you stood at the rail exchanging mirthful curses
with a man whose one good eye could unerringly spy
the seam in a tightly sealed oyster's shell,
and the lemon juice squeezed and rubbed onto
working hands to eradicate the smell of sucking on
and swallowing warm crawfish washed down
with quarts of cold beer, or the two huge italians
that had a grill called pennies where
the sizzling hot sausage was so good, so hot
the cap never had to come off the tabasco bottle,
and the french bread was fresh and the lettuce crisp
and the tomatoes so sweet you lifted a slice
and slid it into your mouth grinning in delight
at the wonderfully tart taste bursting forth,
alerting your salivary glands to the po-boy treat
shortly to follow;

where music factories called nightclubs
and music emporiums better known as joints
like the fabled club 77 at which the sunday night sets

lasted till monday morning where from
some patrons would head straight to work
without seeing their homes, which they had left
on saturday not to return until late after-work
on monday where upon one fell out totally oblivious
to anything until tuesday morning,
hang-outs and haunts in which a young man
feeling himself saw a fine woman from the rear,
figuring that was all he needed to know,
rushed over to her, tapped her on the shoulder
and was semi-shocked to see, when she turned around,
that this fox was his twelfth-grade teacher,
and though clearly a bit embarrassed,
neither of them was really surprised
that the other was there;

where protest marches and marcus garvey celebrations,
spring festival carriage and limousine parades
with little freckled-faced future creole queens shyly waved
a gloved hand at ruffians with holes in their pants
as their manhood throbbed at the thought of
knocking the little man out of those young girl's boats;

where tambourines fanned us, sudan regaled us,
and the avenue steppers showed how our feet
would not fail us as long as we stuck one to the other
high stepping and kicking up dust, all up
and down the way with everyone on the one
and yet at the very same time each and all of us,
the young, old, short and tall of us,
exactly and precisely doin' what we wanna
and only what we wanna;

where fleets of second-liners have carried so many of us
off to the great beyond in ceremonies during which
coffins were sat on bars and shots of scotch were poured atop
the casket, a libational commemoration of another man
who done gone to glory or how the unforgettably gorgeous
sight of a mother dancing atop the box that held the remains
of her son was a socially sanctioned and totally acceptable
way to both memorialize a life as well as say her last goodbyes
   accompanied by the bravado of
some young dimple-cheeked
trumpeter dueling with an elegant grey-bearded cornetist,
the both of them trying to out blow the other,
one could have been named Joshua and
the elder might have been called Gabriel, as their brass notes
rang out the strains of "i'll fly away, oh lordy, i'll fly...";

there, where a once proud avenue is now nothing
but a site of sadness, a cemetery for the rusted corpses
of flooded cars covered only in the flimsiest scrim
of katrina dust caked on like filthy rings
in the toilet bowl of a superdome bathroom;

there, beneath the bridge, on north claiborne avenue.

Chuck Perkins

Street Names

Tchoupitoulas goes to the Market everyday—

He's a fisherman.

After running through Julia and three Greek muses,

He comes to Felicity

Napoleon plows through the Roman Coliseum

Gathering steam at a Camp

Headed straight for Tchoupitoulas

Tchoupitoulas has already heard the muffled submissions to
    Napoleon's fury

After passing through Milan and Constantinople

So he races to warn the Chippewa that they shouldn't cross
    Napoleon

Tchoupitoulas runs up the other side of the river to warn the
    other Chippewa

Instead he runs into Robert, Amelia, Eleanor and Dufossat

Living his version of the movie *Groundhog Day*

Titled, where did all the white people come from?

In New Orleans, Religious run from Nuns
And Saints double cross each other like two bit hustlers.

When St Claude crossed St Philip—
St Philip became so distraught,
He ran straight to Bourbon.

St Claude used to run with good Children

He's a renaissance man

Everyday he's running to Art, Music, Painters, Desire and Piety

Looking for a lost poet hidden beneath a Roch

Every day in New Orleans St Claude runs from a Flood to
        Poland and
France and Spain

MLK meets with the Spanish Governors Galvez and Miro—
They try convincing him they're straight shooters—
But every day they meet St Bernard and end up being crooked.

People are always whispering about the Frenchmen
Well I saw him when he disappeared into the Quarter
And I saw him when he came out—
I can assure you that Frenchmen was never straight.

Jahi Salaam

wake up call

this a dedication—
to the native population
this a wake up call—
to the brainwashed and miseducated
this a wake up call—
to the oppressed and manipulated
divided and conquered,
separated and infiltrated

this ain't what MLK was dreaming bout when he fought for
    integration
we gave up our communities, left ourselves wide open to
    gentrification
caught in a cycle of self hatred, taught to equate black with
    second rate
instead of sticking together, we'd rather try to assimilate

instead of being proud, we'd rather be ashamed
instead of giving back, when we make it, we forget where we
    came from
instead of giving back to the hood, we just take away
and the first chance we get, we take our money and find
    somewhere else to stay

this for treme, where the musicians used to play
before the city started shutting down second line parades
before they redlined us off with the I-10 highway

...

this for the lower nine, where my people used to stay
where the levees always seem to break (1927, hurricane Betsy,
    Katrina)
...
...

this for all our people who couldn't afford to evacuate
stranded with no food and no shelter for days
this for all our people who passed away
this for our people who got shot dead by the national guard
    brigades

this for all the projects that got tore down, where our people
    posed to go
now?
ain't none of this accidental, them devils got it all planned out
downtown, uptown, it's the same story all around ...

in New Orleans and all across the nation, it's the same things
    were facing
modern day enslavement, prison privatization,
colonization,
appropriation,
exploitation,
destabilization,
displacement,
disaster capitalization
...

this for every hood, every ghetto
every barrio, every slum, (and reservation)
this for the whole African diaspora,
never forget where we come from

I sing of far vistas of asphalt streets and highways

Beckoning us on to fantastic future years...

Brenda Marie Osbey

Everything Happens to
(Monk and) Me

for JB Borders IV

we hustle hard as the rest of the folk me and my baby
but it never seems to count.
so
we stop off nights and hear the best and worst of everybody.
my baby's down in heart but that hasn't stopped him yet.
me i'm just down.
we struggle-in.
we sit ourselves down.
we believe in everything.
we know the other life is a club called havana.
we dream in unison how it will be there
and have never had this conversation because we do not need to.
we believe in everything my baby and me.
we *know* that life on the other side is a club called havana
and sometimes we ache for it
but not out loud.

the music in this city is not heard in clubs.
this is not a thing we recite
we know this
by heart.
no.
it's in the thrumming of the empty streetcar tracks
the thrumming of the old wooden banquettes beneath the
      newer cement

it's in the bricks the slaves are cursing over eternally
the way the poorest of the crazies look up from rheumy eyes
the way a workingman hauls his haunches home to his woman
a little low on one side his walk
a little bit too hurried or too slow
for him for her one
the way she doesn't wait but puts his plate over water
pretending to watch the news
washing her hands
or else not stirring
pretending not to daydream
over porkchops and brown gravy

the thrumming is in the way it hangs
the whole city hanging
at the edge of a water no one will wade
the whole city hanging
the way the not-so-young-anymore men used to say
"can you *hang* with that?" and mean it
mean it.
that's the problem with this city
we *all* mean it so hard.
and this is a soft city
a city of softness
turning turning ever on the edge of its own meaning
and hanging on to *us* for dear life.
we really
really
mean
to get it right soon some glorious day some soft thrumming night
and "oh" cry out the pretty little street-stepping-boys sometimes

"ain't we righteous, y'all!"
yes sweetness we mouth in their direction when we hear or see
    or care
we really truly are

and that's what started the whole damn thing to begin with:

me and my baby just want to hear some music from time to
    time.
well i do.
my baby he loves me and sometimes just says okay.
and sometimes he just fakes it like he doesn't have this longing.
my baby thinks he's stoic—
that old negro stoicism sterling loved so.
but no
he wouldn't be so sad around the eyes late evening into night
after supper and before cigarettes
—we still have supper here
and late-night breakfast
and say "good evening" after twelve noon—
he wouldn't have those *eyes*
not from being old-fashioned sterling/negro-stoic
oh-but-no we say here (first syllable stressing)
truth is he's old-fashioned negro-martyr heroic.
i get him.
then i get him out.
we get out into or behind the crowd
we do not need to look at one another
we nod
we hang our hands about as if we've known it all along.
we thrum

we thrum
we thrum
inside the city

at least that's how it is
when we condescend to our hipper selves

"oh baby" we say together later on
"oh
oh, baby"

but ain't we righteous y'all?

and out of nowhere in the night
solo
standards
the funny-sad
the halved
the tired
witty
unlovely chords
and everything within us that ever hoped for hipness stirs.
not following that sound
we laugh into the night
because we were young once
and very very hip.
we were young once
and very very wise.
we were young once
these streets were always ours
we paved them with the flats of our heels

we danced
and never bothered to tire
or if we did it hardly mattered
our hippest coolest livest selves
out late and full up with heart
valiant as the very streets
we wind we wind me and my baby
we reach the other side the place called havana
we reach our own unlovely selves
—bitter chords—
reach for each other
and are wise
enough to know better
our tender places older than before.

it never ends.
we follow the sweep of the river downtown and up.
somewhere is music we can hear
havana and unlovely chords
and tight here with us
the city and the indigo night
its tuneless keyboard silent altogether for the moment
we play upon the night
each key a treasure we have close-*tight* between us
unrighteous
and unlovely
full up with longing
in the streets.

Afterword

Jerry W. Ward, Jr.

This anthology is a post-Katrina metaphor of self, a signifying **of** and **on** the psychological and philosophical dimensions of poetic autobiography. It is a record of how poetic sensibility might choose to deal with multiple traumatic challenges regarding history, location, and the mind/body in pain. As a linguistic proposition, "I Am New Orleans" accords privilege to the radical idea of "collective individuality" and black expressive tradition. "I" is frequently "We" in the matrix, which many African American writers use to represent the complexity of "being-human-in-the-world," thereby inscribing our diasporic authority in time and space during and after the period of American enslavement.

Much to his credit as a poet/historian, Marcus Bruce Christian created the long poem "I Am New Orleans" as a model of intervening in the making of history. On one hand, that poem responded to James Weldon Johnson's call for black poets of the twentieth century to discover the language and forms of racial wisdom, as well as to Jean Toomer's efforts in *Cane* (1923) to rescue a unique history from oblivion. On the other hand, Christian illuminated the possibility of performing an ideology of resistance in making and recording narratives of identity. And following Christian's lead, the contributors to *I Am New Orleans* necessitate our thinking about what indeed matters in the making, unmaking, and remaking of the city as urban and global/local Lebensraum.

The poetry in *I Am New Orleans* is neither obscure nor as transparent as glass, but it does demand that we engage in the saturation richly described in Stephen E. Henderson's

Understanding the New Black Poetry (1973) in its twenty-first-century iterations. Thus, we have the option of reading Rudolph Lewis's multiple introductions to Christian's scholarship and modernist poetics—one version of which can be found in *Dillard Today*[1] and a slightly modified version that is featured in *I Am New Orleans and Other Poems* (1999).[2] We can gain a deeper understanding also of Christian's legacy from Tom Dent's "Marcus B. Christian: A Reminiscence and an Appreciation" (1984)[3] and Violet Harrington Bryan's commentary on Christian's poetry in *The Myth of New Orleans in Literature: Dialogues of Race and Gender* (1993).[4]

And, we can locate in the contemporary selections the influence of Christian's Ur-poem, which brings salty wit, jazz and blues moments, and weighted anaphora into the process of identification and remembering—alongside the implacable influence of the city itself. Let readers plunge into the hermeneutics of now and be renewed by passionate attention to what black poets of New Orleans reveal about the value of speaking the many ways we are, indeed, New Orleans.

---

1 *Dillard Today* 2, no.4 (1999), 21-24.

2 Marcus B. Christian, *I Am New Orleans and Other Poems* (New Orleans: Xavier Review Press, 1999).

3 Tom Dent, "Marcus B. Christian: A Reminiscence and an Appreciation," *Black American Literature Forum* 18, no. 1 (1984): 22-26.

4 Violet Harrington Bryan, *The Myth of New Orleans in Literature: Dialogues of Race and Gender* (Knoxville: University of Tennessee Press, 1993).

Index